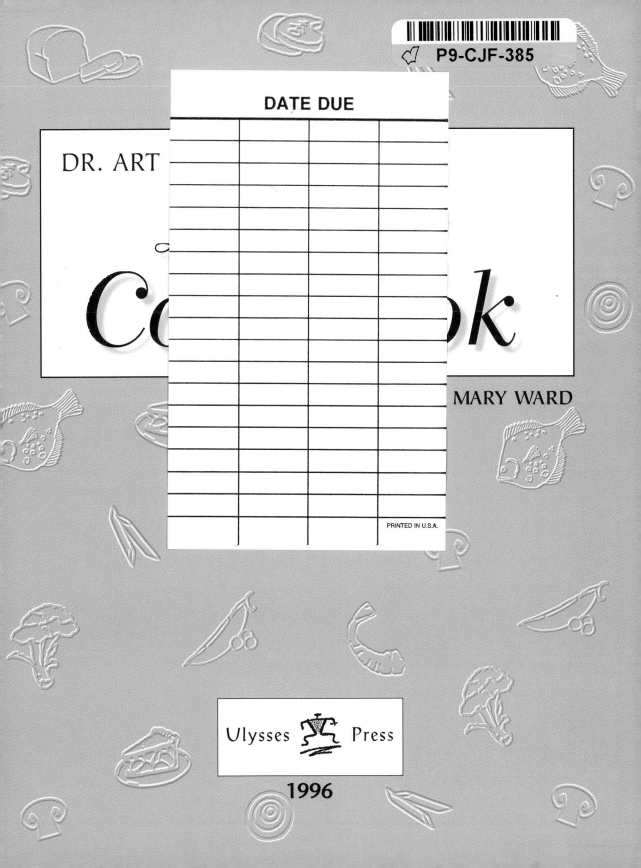

DR. ART

*Co**ok*

MARY WARD

Ulysses Press

1996

Nutritional values for the recipes in this book have been computed using Nutritionist III TM, Version 7.2, First DataBank (formerly N-Squared Computing), San Bruno, California.

Seven recipes in this book are Copyright © 1993 Corning Consumer Products Company, and are reprinted with permission. These recipes include *Baked Tarragon Chicken, Halibut with Confetti Sauce, Papaya Salad, Pasta with Fresh Tomatoes, Ratatouille, Red Beans and Rice* and *Strawberry Tart*.

Photographs by PhotoDisc™ Images © 1996 PhotoDisc, Inc.: cover (see page 116 for recipe) & pages 31-32, 35, 37-38, 42-44, 46, 48, 50-51, 53, 55, 58-59, 62, 111-112, 115-117, 123-124, 126, 159-162, 165 &170.

Photograph on page 166 by George Motz © 1996 Media Content Marketing, Inc.

Photographs on pages 61, 120, 167-169 & 171 © 1993 Amy Reichman, NYC

Book design by Media Content Marketing, 405 Park Ave., New York, NY 10022

Cover design by DesignWorks

Published by Ulysses Press, P.O. Box 3440, Berkeley, CA 94703-3440

Distributed in the United States by Publishers Group West, in Canada by Raincoast Books, and in Great Britain and Europe by World Leisure Marketing

Library of Congress Catalog Number: 96-60080

ISBN: 1-56975-062-9

Printed in the USA by RR Donnelley & Sons Co.

10 9 8 7 6 5 4 3 2 1

Contents

INTRODUCTION

If you are one of those people who associates a low-fat dietary program with deprivation and dullness, get ready for a pleasant surprise. You are about to discover how satisfying and delicious low-fat cooking can be. The following tantalizing recipes will not only excite your taste buds, but they will also help you to reduce the amount of fat you eat – helping you control your weight, decrease your cholesterol and cut your risk of heart disease.

Even more important than the recipes in this book are the principles behind them. As you apply these principles to your cooking on a regular basis, you will understand why cutting down the amount of fat you eat doesn't mean sacrificing good taste. In the pages that follow, you will learn some basic concepts and techniques you can use in all of your meal preparation. Use them to modify your favorite old recipes or to create brand new ones.

What are the scientific reasons behind the shift to low-fat cooking? Actually, in modest amounts, fats are an important element of a well-balanced diet. They are a source of energy, they act as building blocks for vital substances made by the body and they aid in transporting compounds such as fat-soluble vitamins (A, D, E and K) throughout the body. Every cell in your body needs fat, so you must have some fat in your diet to stay healthy.

But Americans eat too much fat – one reason why obesity and high blood cholesterol problems are so common. In fact, fat comprises about 37 percent of the average American's total calories; that's almost twice as much as we recommend to keep your weight and cholesterol level under control. Fats are a much more concentrated source of calories than carbohydrates or protein; each fat gram supplies 9 calories, while a gram of carbohydrate or protein provides only 4 calories. Thus, by shifting to low-fat eating, you can actually eat larger quantities of food without gaining weight or raising your cholesterol level.

Studies have linked high-fat diets not only to heart disease, but also to several types of cancer (of the colon, breast and possibly the ovary, uterus and prostate). High-fat diets contribute to obesity, increasing your risk of developing high blood pressure and diabetes. A low-fat diet can benefit you in many important ways.

There are three types of fat – saturated, monounsaturated and polyunsaturated. Saturated fats are the biggest contributor to heart disease because they raise blood cholesterol levels. But when weight loss is your primary goal, you need to cut back on all three types of fat. They are all 100 percent fat – equally poor choices for someone trying to lose weight. Their chemical structures may differ, but all of them contribute to putting extra fat on your body.

MAKING THE MOST OF THESE RECIPES

The recipes in this book have been carefully developed to help you lower the fat in your diet without giving up the pleasure of eating. To achieve this goal, I called upon Mary Ward to create the recipes. Mary, her husband and their three children have always been committed to a healthy lifestyle. The delectable recipes in this book reflect Mary's lifelong commitment to low-fat, healthy eating, as well as her creative touch.

The ingredients you'll find in these recipes are widely available in most supermarkets. They come from a variety of food groups, and will help you maintain a balanced diet while reducing your fat intake. And if you think that cooking healthy involves more work, think again: these recipes are just as easy to prepare as the high-fat ones you have probably relied on for years.

To help you use these recipes and adapt other recipes in a reduced-fat way, Chapter 1 will present information on how to:
• Substitute more healthful ingredients for those high in fat.
• Extend your favorite dishes with low-fat foods, and enhance them with fat-free and low-fat flavorings and seasonings.
• Alter your cooking techniques to produce healthier dishes.

Once you become familiar with these guidelines, you can apply them to any other cookbook on your kitchen shelf. You don't need to throw out those old recipes; just adapt them in the manner you'll read about here. So turn the page and get started on the path to delicious and healthy dining.

Best wishes for good eating and good health.

Art Ulene, MD

Adapting Recipes for Fat Reduction

As we promised in the Introduction, you don't have to give up taste to reduce the fat in your diet. Lower-fat meals can be delicious and easy to prepare. In this chapter, you'll find specific recommendations for transforming a recipe high in fat into one that is low in fat.

With some smart substitutions, you can continue to use your favorite cookbooks, making them allies in your efforts toward low-fat eating. Some of the changes are obvious, such as substituting nonfat milk for whole milk, roast chicken for fried chicken and jam for butter on your toast. Others may not be quite as evident, but they are just as simple to make. And perhaps surprisingly, the flavor of the original dishes will usually be retained in these recipe makeovers.

NOW LET'S GET DOWN TO SPECIFICS

SUBSTITUTIONS

MEATS

You do not need to completely eliminate red meat from your diet to gain control over your weight. But because meat can be high in fat, you should choose lean cuts. For beef, that means selecting sirloin, round, chuck, loin, flank or extra-lean ground beef. Look for cuts that have the least amount of visible white fat (marbling) in the muscle; streaks of fat indicate a higher-fat cut of meat.

The best pork choices are tenderloin, leg (fresh), shoulder (arm or picnic) and boiled ham. When buying lamb, choose cuts of leg, arm, rib or loin. All trimmed cuts of veal are acceptable, except those that are commercially ground. Also check the grade of meat. The label USDA "select" indicates that the meat is lower in fat than "choice" or "prime"; "select" varieties are also tasty and rich in protein and iron, and thus should be your first choices.

POULTRY

Ounce for ounce, chicken is lower in fat than nearly all cuts of beef, particularly if you remove the skin. So consider poultry as a frequent substitute for meat in your recipes.

Ground or shredded chicken and turkey can be utilized in a number of imaginative ways. For instance, use them (instead of ground beef) to make meatballs, meatloaf, chili, tacos, spaghetti sauce or any of your other favorite ground-beef recipes. Keep in mind, however, that unless you have turkey ground to order, it probably won't be as low in fat as you think. Manufacturers of commercially ground turkey are allowed to grind some of the turkey skin in with the ground turkey, which increases the fat content by as much as 15 percent.

Removing the skin of chicken or turkey before serving is very important, and a way to reduce the amount of fat by more than half. Even if you're already in the habit of taking off the skin, you can lower your fat intake even more by choosing light over dark meat. For example, while 43 percent of the calories of skinless dark chicken meat come from fat, only 23 percent of the calories in skinless light chicken meat are fat calories. Breast meat tends to be the leanest portion of the chicken.

SEAFOOD
Most fish have less fat than red meat and poultry. In general, the fat content of fish with dark flesh is higher than that of fish with lighter flesh. Those particularly low in fat include halibut, cod, sea bass, snapper, haddock, flounder and perch. Many types of shellfish (clams, scallops, crab, lobster) are also quite low in fat. If you buy canned tuna, be sure it is packed in water instead of oil; this can cut the fat content by as much as 80 percent.

CHEESE
As a rule, cheese must be selected carefully and eaten sparingly. Most cheeses are brimming with fat, which makes up a staggering 65 to 75 percent or more of their calories. A single ounce of hard cheese like Swiss contains nearly 8 grams of fat! Even cheese that's labeled "low-fat" or "part-skim" might surprise you. Part-skim ricotta, for example, gets 51 percent of its calories from fat, while reduced-fat mozzarella cheese has a 39 percent fat content. There are about 3 grams of fat in one ounce of reduced-fat mozzarella, which is about the same amount of fat as in a three-ounce portion of skinless, light-meat chicken. Nevertheless, there are ways to reduce your fat intake and still eat cheese.

When you're making substitutions in recipes that call for some of the harder, higher-fat cheeses, for example, using those with strong flavors will allow you to cut down on the amount you use. Also, if you grate cheese, you will probably eat less of it. Grated parmesan, cheddar and sapsago cheeses can be sprinkled on main dishes and casseroles, allowing you to add taste without consuming too much fat. Feta cheese is another good choice, sprinkled in a salad or on top of a casserole. Other acceptable lower-fat substitutions are part-skim mozzarella and Romano; they'll work just as well in your recipes as their higher-fat counterparts.

But remember that hard cheeses should be eaten in limited amounts, even the part-skim varieties.

By the way, there are also many fat-free cheeses now available – containing 0 grams of fat! However, some people are unhappy with the unusual consistency, flavor and texture of nonfat cheeses, preferring instead to use the reduced-fat varieties, but in smaller quantities. Check the labels of the cheeses you're thinking of using and keep this guideline in mind: any cheese with more than 2 grams of total fat per ounce must be eaten sparingly.

OTHER DAIRY PRODUCTS

Milk is an excellent source of protein, vitamins and minerals in every gulp. But you've got to be careful about which kind of milk you buy. At first glance, the differences between the varieties of milk – whole milk (3.3 percent fat by weight), low-fat (2 percent or 1 percent), and nonfat or skim (nearly free of fat) – don't seem that dramatic. But calculations by weight can be deceiving. The differences may not seem like much – until you look at grams of fat and calories.

Each cup of whole milk contains just over 8 grams of fat. That adds up to 74 fat calories per cup, which means that 49 percent of the calories in whole milk come from fat. In spite of its name, low-fat (2%) milk still contains almost 5 grams of fat, so 35 percent of its calories come from fat. By contrast, nonfat or skim milk contains less than one-half gram of fat per cup. Clearly, when recipes call for milk, you're much better off choosing nonfat. Nonfat milk works very well in soups, sauces, puddings and baked products. In recipes that call for half-and-half or heavy cream, evaporated skim milk is an excellent alternative. It has the same rich, creamy texture, but only a trace of fat. You can even whip it, but make certain that the milk (as well as the bowl and the beaters) are well chilled before you begin.

Other substitutions in this category are just as easy to make. For example, when a recipe calls for sour cream, try low-fat or nonfat yogurt or yogurt cheese instead; your taste buds probably won't know the difference. A cup of nonfat yogurt has 0 grams of fat, while an equal amount of regular sour cream contains a staggering 42 grams! A combination of cottage cheese and buttermilk works, too. Use yogurt as a topping for chili or baked potatoes, or in place of mayonnaise in a salad dressing. It also makes a flavorful base for a dip. Or try it in place of sour cream in soups and sauces. Be aware, though, that yogurt tends to separate if overheated. To keep that from happening, add the yogurt at the end of the cooking time and warm gently. Or prior to heating, mix one tablespoon of cornstarch into a cup of yogurt.

OILS

If you're concerned about your coronary arteries, you probably already know that you're better off avoiding saturated fats and cooking instead with monounsaturated oils like olive oil and canola oil, or polyunsaturated oils like corn oil and safflower oil. But don't forget: All fats inflict similar damage when your goal is weight control. All oils are 100 percent fat! A single tablespoon of any oil contains about 13.5 grams of fat and about 120 calories – every one of them a fat calorie. So, the less oil you consume, the better.

When recipes call for oil, you can usually reduce the amount you use significantly without hurting the taste and consistency. The key is to cut back slowly – one tablespoon of oil at a time each time you make the recipe, until you notice a real difference. By the way, don't be tempted to pour on a product that advertises itself as "100% vegetable oil," as if that means it's healthy. Although vegetables themselves are generally very low in fat, the same can't be said for vegetable oil, which is 100 percent fat.

USING FOOD EXTENDERS

Food extenders are low-fat ingredients that can be mixed into your favorite dishes; in the process, they will dilute or stretch a main ingredient that is high in fat. That means you can still enjoy the primary ingredient, but each serving will have less fat in it (assuming you keep the portion size constant).

Some of the best food extenders might already be right in your refrigerator. Grains (and products made from grains), vegetables, fruits, beans and lentils all make great extenders – and they've been used successfully this way for centuries. If meat dishes are among your favorites, the addition of these extenders will allow you to reduce the amount of meat (and fat) in your recipes, while still preserving the basic identity of the dish. For instance, by adding grains (rice, barley) or vegetables (potatoes, carrots, tomatoes) to a meat recipe, you won't give up the robust nature of the dish, but your fat intake will decline. In the same way, using beans to replace some of the meat in a chili recipe will lower the amount of fat per serving.

Meat recipes are not the only dishes that can be extended this way. If you're preparing a "creamy" soup, use cooked, pureed vegetables instead of the cream. With a meat-based soup or stew, the addition of beans and lentils will make you forget that you've decreased the amount of meat.

USING FOOD ENHANCERS

Because fat is an important contributor to the flavor of foods, you'll need to compensate for the diminished taste of low-fat dishes by adding other sources of flavor. Food enhancers are low-fat ingredients that are very flavorful. Fresh dried herbs and spices are a good place to start for flavor enhancement. Experiment with a wide variety of them, and find out which ones please your palate most.

Dill and parsley are favorites of many people, particularly on foods such as fish, poultry and vegetables. Enhancers like garlic, ginger, onions and shallots can also make low-fat foods more appealing; for example, just a teaspoon of fresh, chopped herbs can be added to several servings of vegetables, giving their flavor a real boost. To provide extra "bite" for some of your recipes, try adding a little red or green sweet pepper. For an even stronger flavor, rely on hot peppers, salsa, mustard or hot sauce.

Other popular options are wine vinegar, or a mellow vinegar like balsamic. For skinless chicken dishes, spicy marinade can add pungency.

And to garnish salads or rice dishes, bean sprouts – or sprouts from wheat seeds or alfalfa seeds – are excellent choices. When adding flavor to traditional foods like baked potatoes, leave the butter and sour cream in the refrigerator, and choose lower-fat enhancers instead. We already suggested nonfat yogurt as a substitute for sour cream; but to boost the taste of the yogurt, add some fresh dill, parsley, scallions, green pepper or chives. If you want an alternative to yogurt, a few tablespoons of stewed tomatoes or spicy tomato salsa will give baked potatoes a unique flavor, or top the potato with a combination of dried herbs and a small amount of lemon juice. On the topic of lemons, keep a few fresh ones in your refrigerator; a little squeeze can give flavor to all kinds of foods.

While flavor enhancers need not be fresh, people often find it worthwhile to make the extra effort of using fresh ingredients. For example, use a pepper mill for freshly ground black pepper. Other fresh spices – from garlic to ginger root – can be purchased in many grocery stores, and they'll remain fresh for weeks.

COOKING TECHNIQUES FOR LOW-FAT EATING

Your best attempts at choosing low-fat foods can be undermined in the kitchen if you prepare your meals in ways that increase the fat content. You can start with the healthiest ingredients, but if they're cooked improperly, all of your efforts will be sabotaged. To lay claim to a new, fat-reducing style of cooking, here are some important guidelines:

COOKING MEATS, POULTRY AND FISH
Frying: Avoid frying whenever possible. It increases a food's fat content significantly. When you're frying chicken, for instance, some of the oil is absorbed by the chicken. At the same time, the fat within the meat cannot drain away during cooking. By contrast, the alternatives listed below allow the fat to drip off, so it will be lost rather than ending up in your body where it can subvert your weight-loss efforts.

Broiling: Foods that you might have pan-fried in the past should be broiled instead. Meatballs are a good example; when broiled, their fat will drip into the pan below, so you're not frying them in their own fat. Potato slices can also be broiled, creating low-fat French fries; or broil eggplant slices to create eggplant parmigiana.

Roasting: Meats should be roasted in a preheated oven set at about 350° F. That's a temperature low enough to allow the fat to drip off. (At higher temperatures, the meat will be seared, and it will retain the fat.) To keep lean meat moist while cooking, baste it with a fat-free liquid such as fruit juice marinade or soy sauce.

Baking: Although similar to roasting, baking uses a covered container in the oven. This is a particularly good approach for less fatty cuts of meat, but you may need to add some cooking liquid, such as wine, fruit juice or meat and/or vegetable stock.

Poaching: This is a good choice for cooking fish. You don't need a special fish poacher to use this technique; a regular skillet will work just as well. Make sure you add enough liquid (broth, wine, water seasoned with lemon or dill) to completely cover the fish. Cook until the fish is fork-tender.

Steaming: Try steaming fish in a steamer basket placed in a pan large enough to accommodate it. Put some water – seasoned with herbs, wine or other flavorings – into the pan, and then insert the steamer with the fish in it. The cooking time should be about one minute for each ounce of fish.

Sautéing: When a recipe recommends sautéing, you'll usually cut the food into small pieces and cook it uncovered over high heat. Instead of cooking in oils or fats, try liquids such as wine, flavored vinegar, unsweetened fruit juice or defatted chicken (or vegetable) broth. Or coat the pan with a vegetable oil spray. (These sprays are now marketed with flavors of their own, such as olive oil or butter flavoring.)

COOKING VEGETABLES, LEGUMES AND LENTILS

Vegetables contain very little fat, and your goal should be to keep them that way. Avoid the temptation to cook them in butter or oils, or to smother them with high-fat sauces. Also, select from the cooking techniques outlined below that preserve as much of the natural nutrition of these foods as possible.

Steaming: Although boiling is a common way to cook vegetables, many vitamins and minerals are lost in the process. This depletion of nutrients is much less likely to occur with steaming. Put vegetables in a steamer basket once the water (about 1 inch deep) is boiling; after the vegetables are in place, reduce the heat so the water is simmering. Place the lid on the pot, making sure that the water does not touch the food during cooking. When the vegetables start to become tender – but still retain some crispness – they are ready to eat. The usual cooking time is 5 minutes for most vegetables cut in serving sizes.

Stir-frying: When you stir-fry vegetables, which involves cooking them in very intense heat, they retain their color, texture and nutrients. There's another advantage as well: Only a little bit of oil is needed to stir-fry. Even better, try using small amounts of broth, wine or lemon juice. Pour the liquid around the edges of the wok (or heavy skillet), and once it is hot, place the vegetables (sliced, diced or minced) into it. Stir the food constantly, making sure it is slightly coated to seal in the juices. You may need to add more liquid before cooking is complete.

Microwaving: Like steaming, microwave cooking keeps vitamin loss to a minimum. Follow the instructions that come with your oven for specific cooking times.

USING COOKING OILS

As you've already read, oils – whether saturated, polyunsaturated or monounsaturated – are all the same when it comes to caloric content and weight control. So, although you'd lean toward an unsaturated fat when trying to protect your coronary arteries, all cooking oils are on a level playing field when you're attempting to shed excess pounds. Look for alternatives to oils whenever you can. You can cut the amount of fat in your dishes by using non-stick vegetable oil cooking spray or non-stick cookware. If you use conventional oil, don't pour it into your pan; instead, apply it with a brush to avoid using too much. All you need is a very thin coat, just enough to keep the food from sticking.

ADDITIONAL WAYS TO TRIM AND SKIM OFF EXCESS FAT

■ Trim away all visible fat before cooking meat. Because you can't cut out the fat within the meat, be especially conscientious about buying the leanest cuts possible.

■ With poultry, remove not only the skin, but all of the visible fat as well. If you're convinced that chicken without skin is not worth eating, try the following: Dip the skinless chicken parts in skim milk, and roll them in crushed oat bran cereal to coat the surface. Then bake them and enjoy the tasty results.

■ Soups, stews and sauces should be refrigerated before using, so the fat in them will rise to the top and congeal. You can then easily skim off the fat before reheating. For each tablespoon of fat you remove from the surface, you'll eliminate 120 fat calories.

■ Turn to non-stick cookware. The use of non-stick cookware is one of the most important moves you can make to lower the fat in your diet. This cookware doesn't have to be expensive, but the label does need to say "non-stick coating." For example, substituting a non-stick pan in place of a regular frying pan allows you to sauté with much less oil. In fact, only 2 teaspoons will keep most vegetables from sticking and burning when using a non-stick pan. In most recipes, this will save you over 15 grams of fat.

ADAPTING YOUR RECIPES TO LOWER THE AMOUNT OF FAT

Almost any recipe can be changed to lower its fat level. As a general rule, start cooking with half the fat called for in a recipe. Add more only if you need it (you probably won't!). In most cases, the chemistry of the recipe will not be altered by this fat reduction. Vegetables with strong aromas (such as onions and peppers) can boost the flavor of dishes in which the fat has been minimized.

Let's look at specific examples of how recipes can be adapted in low-fat ways, using many of the approaches we've already described in this chapter. In each case, the recipes on the right side of the page also appear in more detail later in the book, complete with preparation methods. In this section, however, we'll look at how easy it is to take a high-fat recipe and cut its fat significantly.

CHOOSE LOWER-FAT INGREDIENTS

New low- and nonfat food items are being added to supermarket shelves every week – from cheeses to yogurt to pasta. Most of these products are quite good and easy to cook with, although the nonfat cheeses tend to clump rather than melt when cooked. As you shift to low-fat cooking, do some taste testing of your own along the way; trial and error will help you find items and brands that work best for you. When selecting meat, always look for extra-lean ground beef, chicken or turkey. In the following *Pasta with Meat Sauce* recipes, the use of extra lean ground beef – the only change in the ingredient list – reduces total fat by 75 percent.

PASTA WITH MEAT SAUCE

(see recipe on page 181)

REGULAR GROUND BEEF

2 teaspoons olive oil
4 cloves garlic, minced
1 large onion, chopped
1 pound regular ground meat
6 ounces tomato sauce
28 ounces crushed tomatoes
1/2 cup dry red wine
2 tablespoons fresh herbs
1 1/2 pounds pasta, cooked

EXTRA-LEAN GROUND BEEF

2 teaspoons olive oil
4 cloves garlic, minced
1 large onion, chopped
1 pound extra-lean ground beef
6 ounces tomato sauce
28 ounces crushed tomatoes
1/2 cup dry red wine
2 tablespoons fresh herbs
1 1/2 pounds pasta, cooked

SERVES: 10 ═══════ **NUTRITIONAL INFORMATION PER SERVING** ═══════

Calories:	496	Calories:	355
Calories from fat:	30%	Calories from fat:	11%
Total fat:	16 g	Total fat:	4 g

MAKE SAVVY SUBSTITUTIONS

In most recipes, simple low-fat substitutions can make a dramatic difference in your overall fat intake. When the recipe calls for a whole egg, try 2 egg whites. When it calls for cream, choose yogurt, 1% buttermilk or evaporated skim milk instead. When butter, margarine or cooking oil is in the recipe, decrease the amount to 1 to 2 teaspoons. And if ground beef is called for, as in the following recipe, substitute ground turkey breast.

When you dine on these *Mexican Style Meatballs*, you'll never guess that the meat you are eating is ground turkey breast and that the binding agent is egg whites. And look at all the fat you'll save!

MEXICAN STYLE MEATBALLS

(see recipe on page 30)

GROUND BEEF & WHOLE EGG	**GROUND TURKEY BREAST & EGG WHITES**
1 egg	2 egg whites
1 pound ground beef	1 pound ground turkey breast
1/4 cup cilantro, chopped	1/4 cup cilantro, chopped
1 onion, chopped	1 onion, chopped
2 cloves garlic, minced	2 cloves garlic, minced
2 Jalapeño peppers	2 Jalapeño peppers
1/2 teaspoon cumin	1/2 teaspoon cumin
2 large tomatoes	2 large tomatoes
4 ounces green chilies	4 ounces green chilies

SERVES: 4 ══════ **NUTRITIONAL INFORMATION PER SERVING** ══════

Calories:	331	Calories:	146
Calories from fat:	67%	Calories from fat:	15%
Total fat:	25 g	Total fat:	1 g

CHANGE THE PORTION SIZES

If you occasionally want to indulge in a higher fat meat, cut the portion size, and add a low-fat extender such as potatoes, beans, rice or pasta. This strategy is used often in this book so that certain higher fat entrées may be used.

In the following *Traditional Chateaubriand* recipe, on the left side of the page, you will find cream and butter in the potatoes and larger portions of steak. The *Light Chateaubriand,* on the right, uses more potatoes, low-fat ingredients on those potatoes and smaller amounts of tenderloin.

CHATEAUBRIAND

(see recipe on page 109)

TRADITIONAL

2 small potatoes, baked
2 tenderloin steaks, 8 ounces each
baby vegetables
2 tablespoons butter
1/4 cup cream

LIGHT

2 large potatoes, baked
2 tenderloin steaks, 4 ounces each
baby vegetables
1/2 cup low-fat yogurt
herb sprigs

SERVES: 2 === **NUTRITIONAL INFORMATION PER SERVING** ===

Calories:	727	Calories:	495
Calories from fat:	51%	Calories from fat:	16%
Total fat:	42 g	Total fat:	9 g

Use Low-Fat Coatings

Many people think that coatings – such as those used in the *Veal Scaloppine, Turkey Croquettes, Pork Stir-Fry* and *Eggplant Parmigiana* recipes in this book – are strictly taboo for low-fat cooking. Not true. For coating, try using flour, followed by an egg white binder and then bread crumbs. The egg white binder will become crisp as it cooks, and the bread crumbs will end up with a crunch of their own. Use only a tiny bit of fat and a non-stick frying pan.

Here are high- and low-fat *Eggplant Parmigiana* recipes that use flour, egg (or egg whites) and bread crumbs. Notice the impressive difference in total fat content between them.

EGGPLANT PARMIGIANA

(see recipe on page 195)

HIGH-FAT EGGPLANT PARMIGIANA	LOW-FAT EGGPLANT PARMIGIANA
1 large eggplant (2 pounds)	1 large eggplant (2 pounds)
1 cup all-purpose flour	1 cup all-purpose flour
1 cup bread crumbs	1 cup bread crumbs
1/2 cup grated parmesan cheese	1/4 cup grated parmesan cheese
2 cloves garlic, minced	2 cloves garlic, minced
1 cup oil	2 tablespoons oil
1 cup mozzarella cheese, shredded	1/2 cup mozzarella cheese, shredded
4 whole eggs	1 egg
	4 egg whites
Fry in oil; then bake.	Sauté in a little oil; then bake.

SERVES: 6 ═══ **NUTRITIONAL INFORMATION PER SERVING** ═══

Calories:	855	Calories:	442
Calories from fat:	51%	Calories from fat:	18%
Total fat:	49 g	Total fat:	9 g

OTHER HINTS FOR REDUCING FAT IN YOUR DIET

Don't be locked into traditional thinking about certain foods and dishes. For example, you can approach meat as a flavoring instead of a staple. In most recipes, you can cut the amount of meat in half, while increasing vegetables or carbohydrates at the same time.

MEAT-RELATED TIPS:
■ When a recipe includes bacon, either eliminate it entirely or decrease it considerably. If the recipe calls for 1 pound of bacon, use no more than 1/4 pound. When you cook the bacon, either microwave it until crisp or fry it until very crisp. Drain it to make sure all external fat has been removed. In a bacon, lettuce and tomato sandwich, use just 1 slice of bacon, and crumble it on top of the tomato to make it stretch.

■ The longer you cook meat, the more fat it will lose. So meat that is cooked medium or well-done will typically end up with less fat than meat served rare. By the way, lean cuts tend to cook more rapidly than fattier beef, requiring about 20 percent less cooking time.

■ Non-oil marinades tend to have a pleasant, light and herbal quality. For meat, a tenderizer (wine or fruit juice) plus stock and herbs makes a great marinade. A good rule of thumb is to use 50 percent wine or fruit juice and 50 percent stock.

■ Be creative in your use of oil and butter in order to keep your fat consumption to a minimum. You may believe, for instance, that a bechamel (or white) sauce needs equal proportions of fat and flour – about 2 tablespoons of each for every cup of water – but this isn't true. A delicious sauce can be made from 1/4 cup of flour, cornstarch or arrowroot blended with water, milk or stock. In the case of certain bland sauces, such as the gravy for the *Turkey Croquettes* (see recipe on page 133), a little pat of butter or a splash of a delicious olive oil rounds out the sauce and provides good texture.

VEGETABLE, LEGUME AND FRUIT-RELATED TIPS:
■ With even a tiny amount of fat and a non-stick pan, foods can be browned. When foods that naturally contain some sugar (tomatoes,

onions) are browned intensely, a dark, caramel-like substance will form, creating delicious, interesting flavors.

If you are using tomato paste or sauce in a recipe, try this: Rub the tomato paste around the bottom of a non-stick pan. Heat the pan until it's very hot. When the paste starts to brown and blacken, remove the pan from the heat source. Add a flavorful stock, vegetable water or wine to collect the flavorful bits, and continue with the recipe.

■ The use of vegetable waters is a low-fat cooking technique adopted with great success by many chefs. It simply requires draining the vegetables and saving their water. This water may be added to stock, used in place of stock in your favorite recipes or reduced and used as gravy.

■ To create vegetable water (as in the *Capellini la Checca* recipe on page 177), chop juicy vegetables such as cucumber, zucchini, tomatillos and onion with a couple of ripe tomatoes. Add a teaspoon of salt and allow to sit for several hours. The flavorful water may be used as a base for dressing pasta or as a sauce base.

■ When certain foods are covered while cooking for long periods of time, they break down in ways that create a soft, flavorful stew. This stewing brings out hidden flavors with no additional fat. For instance, in recipes using beans, try cooking the beans to the point where they begin to break down, thus providing their own flavorful "gravy." Summer squashes can be blended with oregano and basil and then stewed; they'll produce a delicious paste that can be used on pasta, as a topping for pizza or as a sandwich filling.

■ Eliminate butter on the dinner table. When choosing a spread for bread or rolls, use jam or jelly instead. Toppings for French toast and pancakes need not include butter, either; use applesauce or fresh fruit. See the *Fruit Sauce* recipe on page 43 for a healthy alternative to syrup.

■ When eating a salad, place the low-fat salad dressing on the side and use it sparingly. Or better still, use nonfat dressing or a squeeze of lemon in place of the dressing. When you make your own salad dressing, cut the oil in the recipe by at least half.

■ When snacking, choose low-fat options such as fresh fruit or cut-up raw vegetables. Also, see the recipes on page 38 for *Salsa with Chips* and page 24 for dips made with *Sour Cream Substitute* and *Yogurt Cheese.*

READING THE NEW FOOD LABELS
Since 1994, new "Nutritional Facts" labels have been placed on most food wrappers and packages. When you're trying to determine the fat content of particular items, these uniform and streamlined labels can make this process relatively simple. While there's lots of information on the labels, only a few numbers are important when trying to keep track of the fat in your diet.

■ Look for two values on the labels: Calories (the total calories in the stated serving size) and Calories from Fat (the number of fat calories in the serving size). Take these two figures, and divide the number of calories from fat by the total calories. Then, multiply this result by 100 to change it to a percentage – namely, the percentage of calories that comes from fat. Thus, if a particular food has 250 calories, and 50 calories from fat, divide 50 by 250. Multiply the answer .20 x 100 = 20%. In this example, 20 percent of the calories come from fat. The lower the percentage of fat, the better.

■ If you are trying to lose weight, significantly cut back on the number of foods you consume with fat calories of 30 percent or more, and increase your intake of those with 10 percent fat calories or less. When foods fall into the middle ground – 11 to 29 percent of calories from fat – eat them carefully and thoughtfully.

Appetizers

The appetizer tray is often packed with small treats that are laden with fat. The following recipes cut the fat without sacrificing the flavor of some familiar and some unfamiliar goodies to offer as appetizers or snacks.

SOUR CREAM SUBSTITUTE

With its good dairy texture and flavor, this is an excellent substitute for sour cream in any recipe.

1/4 cup 1% buttermilk   1 teaspoon lemon juice
3/4 cup 1% milk-fat cottage cheese

Place ingredients in blender and process until smooth. Use this for dips, in cooking and in salads.

SERVES: 4		NUTRITIONAL INFORMATION PER SERVING			
Calories	35	Total Fat	< 1 g	Cholesterol	2 mg
Calories from Fat	14%	Saturated Fat	< 1 g	Sodium	188 mg

YOGURT "CHEESE"

Another sour cream substitute with a rich consistency that works especially well in dips.

2 cups nonfat plain yogurt

Place yogurt in strainer or colander lined with a kitchen towel or cheesecloth. Tie together ends of towel or cheesecloth and strain yogurt, hanging it over a bowl. Strain overnight or up to one day, allowing yogurt to lose excess moisture.

The thick yogurt remaining in the towel or cloth is the yogurt "cheese."

SERVES: 3		NUTRITIONAL INFORMATION PER SERVING			
Calories	60	Total Fat	0 g	Cholesterol	0 mg
Calories from Fat	14%	Saturated Fat	0 g	Sodium	85 mg

BAKED NEW POTATOES WITH YOGURT, ONION AND PARSLEY

Serve as directed, or cool and split the potatoes, make a hole in each and pipe dressing into the hole with a pastry tube. Garnish with a tiny bit of red caviar.

24 tiny, blemish-free, red-skinned new potatoes, scrubbed
1 1/2 cups Yogurt Cheese (see recipe on page 24)
1 small red onion, finely minced

3 tablespoons finely chopped parsley
1 tablespoon sweet wine, i.e. Riesling (optional)
salt and pepper to taste

Preheat oven to 350° F. Arrange potatoes in a layer on a baking sheet. Bake until tender, 20 to 30 minutes. Serve immediately or store in an insulated container for up to 6 hours.

To Serve: Blend yogurt cheese with onion, parsley and sweet wine. Season. Place yogurt dressing in a large bowl with potatoes surrounding it.

Quick and Easy: Use low-fat sour cream substitute to replace yogurt cheese.

SERVES: 24 ═══ **NUTRITIONAL INFORMATION PER SERVING*** ═══

Calories	35	Total Fat	< 1 g	Cholesterol	1 mg
Calories from Fat	7%	Saturated Fat	< 1 g	Sodium	13 mg

* Nutritional information based on appetizer-sized servings

BAYOU SHRIMP REMOULADE

A filling and nutritious appetizer that you can prepare up to 2 days in advance.

1/3 cup tarragon vinegar
1 tablespoon catsup
2 tablespoons freshly
  grated horseradish
  (or prepared horseradish sauce)
1 teaspoon prepared mustard
2 teaspoons Cajun seasoning
4 scallions, with tops, sliced

2 large tomatoes, chopped
1 1/4 cups celery, chopped
1 pound medium-sized cooked,
  cleaned shrimp
6 cups shredded salad greens
  (leaf lettuce, romaine lettuce,
  bibb lettuce)

In a medium-sized bowl, combine and whisk the vinegar, catsup, horseradish, mustard, Cajun seasoning and scallions. Add tomatoes, celery and shrimp and stir to coat. Marinate in refrigerator for 4 to 5 hours.

To Serve: Arrange 1 cup lettuce on each of the 6 salad plates. Spoon the shrimp and sauce over lettuce.

SERVES: 6 ═══════ **NUTRITIONAL INFORMATION PER SERVING** ═══════

Calories	109	Total Fat	1 g	Cholesterol	147 mg
Calories from Fat	7%	Saturated Fat	< 1 g	Sodium	215 mg

DILLED GRAVLAX ON WHOLE WHEAT MELBA

With their festive appearance, these make a great choice for holiday entertaining. Always buy the best quality smoked salmon available.

1 whole-wheat baguette, sliced into
   very thin slices (48 rounds)
1 tablespoon olive oil
   (or a mixture of olive oil and hot oil)
1 tablespoon sesame seeds
8 ounces smoked salmon
8 ounces evaporated skim milk

1 teaspoon lemon juice or orange juice
2 to 3 tablespoons horseradish
1 8-ounce package reduced-fat
   cream cheese, softened
1/4 cup fresh dill (or 2 tablespoons dry)
fresh dill and pimiento for garnish

To make melba, preheat oven to 250° F. Place baguette slices on a cookie sheet. Brush a tiny bit of oil onto each one. Sprinkle with sesame seeds. Bake 1 hour. Store in a tightly sealed plastic bag. In a food processor fitted with a steel blade, chop salmon finely (or finely chop by hand). Add milk in a steady stream until all is absorbed. Add lemon juice, horseradish, cream cheese and dill and blend until combined. Chill for at least 1 hour.

To Serve: Divide mixture among whole-wheat rounds. Garnish with a little dill and pimiento.

Quick and Easy: Use commercially prepared onion melba rounds.

SERVES: 24		NUTRITIONAL INFORMATION PER SERVING*			
Calories	84	Total Fat	2 g	Cholesterol	3 mg
Calories from Fat	20%	Saturated Fat	< 1 g	Sodium	203 mg

* Nutritional information based on appetizer-sized servings

HUMMUS

Quick and easy to make. The secret to a great-tasting hummus is its richly toasted sesame seeds.

1/4 cup sesame seeds	1 teaspoon salt
1 15-ounce can garbanzo beans with liquid	1 small onion, chopped
	sesame seeds for garnish
1 clove garlic, sliced into 3 pieces	chopped green onions for garnish
1 freshly squeezed lemon or 3 tablespoons lemon juice	8 pita rounds, separated and toasted

In a small skillet, toast sesame seeds over high heat. Stir and shake pan as it heats to evenly toast sesame seeds.

Place sesame seeds in a blender. Add remaining ingredients, cover and process on low for 30 seconds. Uncover and stir. Blend on high for 1 minute or until the mixture is smooth.

To Serve: Pour into a decorative 2-cup bowl. Garnish with remaining sesame seeds and chopped green onions. Serve with toasted pita bread or a variety of vegetable crudités and melba rounds.

SERVES: 8 ══════ **NUTRITIONAL INFORMATION PER SERVING** ═════

Calories	151	Total Fat	3 g	Cholesterol	0 mg
Calories from Fat	19%	Saturated Fat	< 1 g	Sodium	640 mg

MARINATED PORK STICKS

This recipe originated in the Philippines and may be used as a main course, served with rice.

1 tablespoon low-fat peanut butter
1 cup chicken stock
1/4 cup light soy sauce
4 cloves garlic
1/2 teaspoon freshly ground pepper

2 pounds pork tenderloin,
    trimmed of any fat
24 4-inch bamboo sticks
12 tiny pita rounds

Place peanut butter, chicken stock, soy sauce, garlic and pepper in a blender. Blend until smooth.

Slice meat into 24 strips about 1/2-inch wide by 4 to 5 inches long. Skewer meat strips in zigzag fashion on bamboo sticks. Place sticks in a plastic bag and pour marinade over all. Marinate overnight or for at least 3 hours.

Heat charcoal or other grill to medium hot. Grill sticks for 5 minutes per side, basting with marinade.

To Serve: Let guests make their own tiny pita sandwiches, by sliding 2 sticks into each piece of pita.

Quick and Easy: Use well-trimmed, precut stir-fry pork.

SERVES: 12 ═══ **NUTRITIONAL INFORMATION PER SERVING*** ═══

| Calories | 157 | Total Fat | 3 g | Cholesterol | 53 mg |
| Calories from Fat | 19% | Saturated Fat | 1 g | Sodium | 389 mg |

* Nutritional information based on appetizer-sized servings

MEXICAN STYLE MEATBALLS

Ground turkey teamed with Mexican spices makes a wonderfully nutritious treat that can be prepared in the microwave!

Meatballs
1 pound ground turkey breast meat
2 egg whites
1/4 cup cilantro, chopped
1 medium-sized onion, chopped
2 cloves garlic, minced
2 fresh or canned Jalapeño peppers,
　 medium or hot, chopped
1/2 teaspoon cumin

Salsa
2 large tomatoes
1 4-ounce can green chilies, diced
1/2 cup cilantro, chopped
1 teaspoon salt

Combine the ground turkey with the egg whites, cilantro, onion, garlic, Jalapeño peppers and cumin. Mix with hands until the mixture holds together well.

Form into 2 to 3 dozen meatballs. Place the meatballs on a microwave-safe tray, and microwave on high for 10 to 12 minutes or until the meatballs are cooked and firm. Turn the tray frequently. Remove the meatballs to a serving platter, discarding the fat. (If using a conventional oven, bake the meatballs on a jelly roll pan at 350° F for 30 minutes.)

Meanwhile, make the salsa in a blender or food processor by processing the tomatoes, canned chilies, cilantro and salt until very smooth.

Place salsa in a 2-cup microwave bowl and microwave on high for 3 minutes, just until hot. Spoon the hot salsa over meatballs and serve immediately. (If using conventional method, heat salsa and meatballs in a saucepan on stove for 5 minutes, stirring occasionally.)

SERVES: 4 ═══ **NUTRITIONAL INFORMATION PER SERVING** ═══

Calories	146	Total Fat	1 g	Cholesterol	70 mg
Calories from Fat	15%	Saturated Fat	< 1 g	Sodium	425 mg

PIZZA ON THE GRILL WITH ROASTED PEPPERS AND THREE CHEESES

Pizza is quick, easy and nutritious. In this recipe, the roasted peppers give it color as well as flavor. Try other toppings such as zucchini and chopped olives, sliced tomatoes and garlic, or a very light coating of basil pesto.

1 package (1/4 ounce) active dry yeast
3/4 cup very warm water
2 cups flour (a blend of wheat, white, cornmeal and bread flour)
1 teaspoon salt
1/2 teaspoon sugar
oil and cornmeal for pizza pans

2 cups roasted red, green and yellow pepper strips
2 ounces low-fat mozzarella cheese, shredded
1/4 cup Parmesan cheese, grated
1/4 cup Romano cheese, grated

Blend yeast with water and allow to rest for 5 minutes. Add flour, salt and sugar, and mix until dough is shiny and firm, about 5 minutes. (This may be done in a food processor or mixer fitted with a dough hook.) Cover dough with a damp cloth and allow to rise in a warm place for 10 minutes.

Preheat oven to 500° F (or heat charcoal grill very hot). Divide dough and roll into 2 10-inch rounds. Place on 2 10-inch pizza pans which have been oiled and sprinkled with cornmeal.

Top the dough with peppers and cheeses. Place in hot oven (or onto grill) and bake 5 minutes or until dough is just set. Slide pizza directly onto oven rack (or grill rack) and continue baking for 5 to 7 minutes until crust is nicely browned and cheeses are melted. Cut each pizza into 6 slices and serve.

Quick and Easy: Use frozen bread or pizza dough.

SERVES: 12 ══════ NUTRITIONAL INFORMATION PER SERVING ══════

Calories	129	Total Fat	3 g	Cholesterol	6 mg
Calories from Fat	20%	Saturated Fat	2 g	Sodium	297 mg

PISSALADIERE

The name Pissaladiere refers to food served on a crust. The flavors come from the blend of vegetables and herbs. This one serves a crowd!

2 packages (1/4-ounce each)
　　active dry yeast
1 1/2 cups very warm water
3 1/2 cups white flour
　　(or a combination of white,
　　wheat and bread flour)
2 teaspoons salt
1 egg, beaten

Topping
3 pounds onions, peeled and chopped
2 tablespoons olive oil
8 ripe tomatoes (or 1 28-ounce can
　　plum tomatoes, drained)
2 cloves garlic, chopped
1/3 cup black olives,
　　chopped (optional)
salt and pepper to taste
fresh herb leaves for garnish, such as
　　basil and parsley

In a medium bowl, dissolve yeast in water. Blend flour, salt and egg, then add yeast mixture to it. Knead until smooth and satiny, adding more water if necessary. Shape dough into a ball, place in a floured bowl or pan, cover with a towel and let rise for 1 hour.

To make topping, cook the onions in oil over low heat until soft and golden, about 45 minutes. Do not brown. Add tomatoes and garlic and cook until water is evaporated. Season with salt and pepper.

Preheat oven to 400° F. Grease a large, 11 x 17-inch cookie sheet. Roll out dough to fit cookie sheet. Spoon on topping and sprinkle with olives. Allow to rise for 15 minutes. Bake at 400° F for 20 minutes, then reduce to 350° F for 20 minutes or until crust is done. Serve warm or at room temperature on a platter garnished with fresh herbs, such as basil and parsley.

Quick and Easy: Use 2 loaves frozen prepared bread dough in place of above crust.

SERVES: 24 ===== **NUTRITIONAL INFORMATION PER SERVING*** =====

| Calories | 112 | Total Fat | 2 g | Cholesterol | 0 mg |
| Calories from Fat | 16% | Saturated Fat | < 1 g | Sodium | 122 mg |

* Nutritional information based on appetizer-sized servings with black olives.

SPRING ROLLS

Baking spring rolls is much healthier than deep frying them and it allows the taste and crunch of the filling to really come through.

8 ounces cooked chicken
  breast, shredded
2 tablespoons soy sauce
1 egg white
1 tablespoon cornstarch
2 tablespoons chicken stock

2 cups finely chopped vegetables
  (include garlic, scallions,
  mushrooms, bean sprouts, pea pods,
  celery, bok choy)
8 egg roll wraps
non-stick cooking spray
teriyaki and mustard dipping sauces

Blend chicken with soy sauce, egg white and cornstarch. Heat chicken stock in a non-stick frying pan. Add chicken mixture and sauté chicken. Add vegetables. Cook until vegetables are tender but crisp.

Portion 1/8 of mixture diagonally into each egg roll wrap. Fold in corners at each end of filling, then roll. Preheat oven to 375° F. Coat a baking tray with non-stick cooking spray. Place egg rolls in pan and bake 15 minutes, until brown.

To Serve: Place on individual plates with small ramekins of teriyaki and mustard dipping sauces.

SERVES: 8 ══ **NUTRITIONAL INFORMATION PER SERVING** ══

Calories	100	Total Fat	1 g	Cholesterol	22 mg
Calories from Fat	9%	Saturated Fat	< 1 g	Sodium	310 mg

VEGETABLE CAVIAR

Black olives are full of fat but used in small amounts, they add a meat-like texture to a dish. They are used well in this recipe.

2 ounces ripe olives, chopped
  and drained
8 ounces green chilies
  (mild or hot), chopped
1/4 cup cilantro, chopped
2 large, ripe tomatoes,
  seeded and chopped

1/4 cup cucumber, peeled and chopped
1/4 cup scallions, sliced
2 teaspoons balsamic vinegar
salt to taste
cilantro sprigs for garnish
8 ounces baked tortilla chips

Combine all ingredients.

To Serve: Drain off excess liquid, garnish with cilantro sprigs and serve with tortilla chips.

SERVES: 8 ━━━━━━━ **NUTRITIONAL INFORMATION PER SERVING** ━━━━━━━

Calories	92	Total Fat	2 g	Cholesterol	0 mg
Calories from Fat	20%	Saturated Fat	< 1 g	Sodium	533 mg

STEAMED CLAMS OR MUSSELS

A recipe that is so simple yet so tasty and nutritious. Serve with plenty of bread to sop up the delicious garlic sauce.

2 pounds clams or mussels
  (or a combination)
1 cup dry white wine
1 cup onion, chopped
2 cloves garlic, chopped

1 cup celery, chopped
4 tablespoons chopped fresh
  oregano (or parsley)
few sprigs oregano for garnish
8 slices crusty Italian bread

Scrub clams or mussels. Discard any that are open. In a large pot, simmer wine and other ingredients for 20 minutes so that flavors blend. Add clams or mussels and steam until all are open, about 5 minutes.

To Serve: Divide clams among four deep bowls, including broth with each. Garnish with oregano and serve with Italian bread rounds.

SERVES: 4 **NUTRITIONAL INFORMATION PER SERVING**

Calories	168	Total Fat	1 g	Cholesterol	29 mg
Calories from Fat	5%	Saturated Fat	< 1 g	Sodium	227 mg

TOMATO OR CUCUMBER
SALSA WITH CHIPS

Homemade salsa is very nutritious, packed with vitamin A, vitamin C and fiber. It's delicious.

10 corn tortillas
2 very ripe large tomatoes
   (or 2 large cucumbers, peeled)
1/2 cup fresh cilantro

2 tablespoons Jalapeño
   peppers, chopped
1/4 teaspoon salt

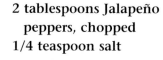

Preheat oven to 400° F. Cut each tortilla into 8 pieces. Place on an ungreased cookie sheet. Bake 15 minutes or until the chips are browned and crisp. Cool.

Cut the tomatoes into 8 wedges. Place tomatoes in a blender along with cilantro, Jalapeños and the salt. Pulse several times until salsa is very smooth, about 1 minute. Serve immediately or store in refrigerator.

Quick and Easy: Use commercially prepared, baked tortilla chips.

SERVES: 10 NUTRITIONAL INFORMATION PER SERVING

| Calories | 74 | Total Fat | 1 g | Cholesterol | 0 mg |
| Calories from Fat | 15% | Saturated Fat | < 1 g | Sodium | 135 mg |

HONEY CHICKEN BITES

These delicious bites always bring rave reviews.

2 whole chicken breasts, boned and
  skinned (about 1 pound)
6 tablespoons honey
2 tablespoons teriyaki marinade

1 teaspoon seasoned salt
1 clove garlic, minced
juice of 1 lime

Blend honey with marinade, salt, garlic and lime juice. Pour over chicken pieces and marinate a few hours or overnight

Preheat oven to 350° F. Cut each boned breast into bite-sized pieces or slice them into 4 x 1-inch strips and skewer them on 6-inch bamboo sticks. Bake 30 minutes, turning once to brown evenly.

To Serve: Place on tiny crackers garnished with herbs, on a leaf of French endive or on a tray with snow peas.

SERVES: 12 ═══════════ **NUTRITIONAL INFORMATION PER SERVING*** ═══════════

Calories	58	Total Fat	< 1 g	Cholesterol	11 mg
Calories from Fat	8%	Saturated Fat	< 1 g	Sodium	99 mg

* Nutritional information based on appetizer-sized servings

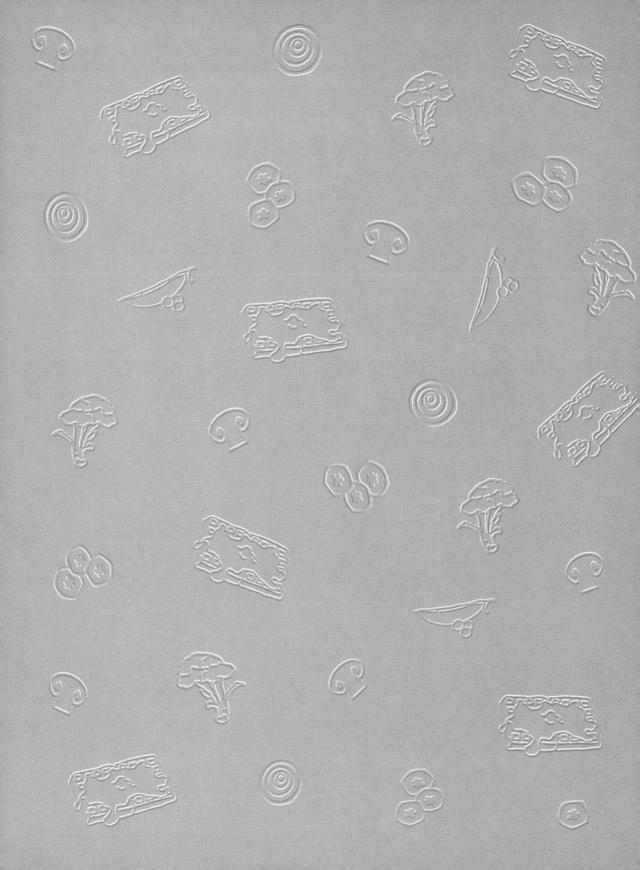

Breakfast

A great variety of foods find their way to the breakfast table. From hearty dishes like corned beef hash to light and frothy fruit drinks, there is something healthfully delicious for every taste in this chapter.

APPLE WAFFLES WITH FRUIT SAUCE

These waffles are best when made in a Belgian waffle iron, although any waffle iron will do.

1 package (1/4 ounce) active dry yeast
1/2 cup very warm water (115° F)
non-stick cooking spray
3 1/2 cups white or wheat flour
1 teaspoon baking powder
1/3 cup light brown sugar, packed

3/4 teaspoon salt
1 cup apple juice, room temperature
4 large egg whites
1 tablespoon oil
1 to 2 cups water

Blend the yeast with very warm water. Set mixture aside for 5 minutes until the yeast is bubbly. Spray the grids of the waffle iron with non-stick cooking spray and preheat for 10 minutes.

In a medium-sized bowl, blend the flour with baking powder, brown sugar and salt. In a large bowl, mix the apple juice with the egg whites and oil. Add the yeast to the apple juice mixture and gently fold in the flour mixture. Allow to rise in a warm place for 15 minutes. Just before baking waffles, add 1 to 2 cups water to make the waffles thick, but pourable. Place 1/2 cup of the waffle batter into each side of the Belgian waffle maker. Spread the mixture with a spatula so that it covers the waffle grid.

Close the lid and allow the waffle to bake until no more steam rises from the waffle maker, about 5 to 8 minutes. When you open the waffle maker, the waffles should release easily. Serve the waffles hot with *Fruit Sauce* (see recipe on page 43) or serve cold with fruit, frozen nonfat yogurt or low-fat cottage cheese.

Belgian waffles can be stored frozen for up to 3 months or refrigerated for 3 weeks. To reheat, microwave each waffle on high for 30 seconds or place waffle in 350° F oven for 5 to 7 minutes.

SERVES: 12	NUTRITIONAL INFORMATION PER SERVING		
Calories	254	Total Fat	3 g	Cholesterol	0 mg
Calories from Fat	10%	Saturated Fat	< 1 g	Sodium	275 mg

FRUIT SAUCE FOR PANCAKES OR WAFFLES

Here's a healthy alternative to heavy or artificially flavored maple syrup.

2 cups fresh or frozen
   strawberries, thawed
1 cup sliced kiwi fruit, peeled
2 ripe bananas
1 cup fresh or frozen
   blueberries, thawed
1/2 cup pure maple syrup
1 cup water

Place all ingredients in a blender. Process until the ingredients are smoothly blended. Heat, if desired, and serve over hot pancakes or waffles. Freeze leftover sauce and reheat it when needed.

SERVES: 12	NUTRITIONAL INFORMATION PER SERVING		
Calories	78	Total Fat	< 1 g	Cholesterol	0 mg
Calories from Fat	4%	Saturated Fat	< 1 g	Sodium	10 mg

STRAWBERRY SMOOTHIE

Here's breakfast in a glass – it's rich in fiber and vitamins, and moderate in calories.

1/2 cup orange juice, fresh or frozen
1 very ripe banana
1 cup fresh or frozen
　(unsweetened) strawberries

1/2 cup nonfat milk
1 cup ice cubes
　(if using frozen strawberries,
　use water instead of ice cubes)

Place the orange juice, banana, strawberries, milk and ice cubes in a blender. Blend until smooth, about 30 seconds. Pour into two 12-ounce glasses. Serve immediately.

SERVES: 2 ══════ **NUTRITIONAL INFORMATION PER SERVING** ══════

Calories	176	Total Fat	1 g	Cholesterol	1 mg
Calories from Fat	< 5%	Saturated Fat	< 1 g	Sodium	34 mg

FROZEN PINEAPPLE REFRESHER

A refreshing way to start the day – low-fat, low calorie and high fiber.

1 cup fresh pineapple pieces
　(or canned or frozen)
1/2 cup orange juice
1 banana
1 cup ice cubes
1 cup club soda

Place pineapple, orange juice, banana and ice cubes in a blender. Blend until smooth, about 30 seconds. Pour into two 16-ounce glasses. Stir in club soda and serve.

SERVES: 2 ══════ **NUTRITIONAL INFORMATION PER SERVING** ══════

Calories	118	Total Fat	< 1 g	Cholesterol	0 mg
Calories from Fat	5%	Saturated Fat	< 1 g	Sodium	27 mg

APPLE BERRY FIZZ

A complete breakfast rich with dietary fiber, served up in a glass.

1 cup canned apple juice
1/2 cup strawberries or raspberries,
  fresh or frozen

1/2 cup ice cubes (if using frozen
  berries, use water instead of ice cubes)
1/2 cup club soda

Place the apple juice, berries and ice cubes or water into a blender. Blend until smooth, about 30 seconds. Pour into a 16-ounce glass. Stir in club soda and serve immediately.

SERVES: 1		NUTRITIONAL INFORMATION PER SERVING			
Calories	161	Total Fat	< 1 g	Cholesterol	0 mg
Calories from Fat	5%	Saturated Fat	< 1 g	Sodium	58 mg

CORNED BEEF HASH

Cut the fat from corned beef hash and keep it a part of your special weekend breakfast.

2 cups beef stock
1/2 cup onion, chopped
1/2 green pepper, seeded and diced
1 rib celery, chopped
1 clove garlic, minced

4 ounces very lean, sliced corned beef,
  finely shredded
2 medium-sized baking potatoes,
  baked and diced

Preheat broiler. In a large non-stick skillet, heat stock. Add onion, pepper, celery and garlic and poach until vegetables are tender. Add corned beef and potatoes and poach until all liquid is absorbed. Broil corned beef hash about 4 inches from broiler heat for a few minutes to crisp. Cut into 4 wedges and serve immediately.

Leftovers are excellent when reheated at 400° F for 20 minutes.

SERVES: 4		NUTRITIONAL INFORMATION PER SERVING			
Calories	143	Total Fat	3 g	Cholesterol	18 mg
Calories from Fat	19%	Saturated Fat	1 g	Sodium	332 mg

FRUIT COMPOTE

A true fruit compote needs five different fruits. You may choose fruits that are fresh, canned, frozen or create your own mixture.

1 cup fresh strawberries, sliced
1 banana, sliced
1 orange, peeled and segmented

2 kiwis, peeled and sliced
1 apple, cut into chunks

Mix all ingredients together and serve. Leftovers may be blended in the blender for a breakfast drink.

SERVES: 4 ═══ **NUTRITIONAL INFORMATION PER SERVING** ═══

Calories	72	Total Fat	< 1 g	Cholesterol	0 mg
Calories from Fat	1%	Saturated Fat	< 1 g	Sodium	5 mg

FRESH TOASTED GRANOLA

This recipe is an absolute favorite; it's rich with dietary fiber and so delicious that you'll want to make extra to give to your friends!

1 cup oat bran hot cereal, uncooked
2 cups rolled oats
2 tablespoons almonds, sliced
2 tablespoons sunflower seeds
2 tablespoons sesame seeds

1/4 cup nonfat dry milk
2 tablespoons dark brown sugar, packed
1/2 teaspoon cinnamon
1/2 cup maple syrup
1/2 cup seedless raisins

Preheat oven to 300° F.

In a large bowl, combine oat bran, rolled oats, almonds, sunflower seeds, sesame seeds, dry milk, brown sugar and cinnamon. Pour maple syrup over ingredients and blend thoroughly.

Spread granola in a rimmed, ungreased 10 x 15-inch jelly roll pan and bake for 45 minutes, stirring every 10 minutes. It is important to stir the granola every 10 minutes to blend flavors and toast granola evenly. Stir in raisins and bake an extra 10 minutes.

Remove from oven and cool. Store in an airtight container for up to 3 months. Serve 1/2 cup granola with nonfat milk or sprinkle it on nonfat frozen yogurt.

SERVES: 24 ═══ **NUTRITIONAL INFORMATION PER SERVING** ═══

Calories	108	Total Fat	2 g	Cholesterol	1 mg
Calories from Fat	18%	Saturated Fat	< 1 g	Sodium	13 mg

ITALIAN FRITTATA

A delicious and hearty combination of vegetables, eggs, noodles and cheese.

non-stick cooking spray
1 cup zucchini, scrubbed
  and chopped with peel
1/3 cup green pepper, seeded
  and chopped into 1/4-inch chunks
1/3 cup onion, chopped coarsely
1 large tomato, chopped
  into 1/2-inch pieces
1 teaspoon dried oregano

1 tablespoon fresh basil, chopped
  (or 1 teaspoon dried)
1/4 teaspoon black pepper
1/2 cup whole-wheat elbow
  macaroni, cooked
12 egg whites, beaten
2 tablespoons Romano cheese,
  freshly shredded

Spray a large, broiler-safe skillet with non-stick cooking spray. Add zucchini, pepper and onion to skillet and heat to hot on stove. Reduce heat, cover and sauté the zucchini, pepper and onion until tender, about 8 minutes, stirring occasionally. Add chopped tomato. Stir in the oregano, basil, pepper and macaroni.

Preheat broiler. Pour the egg whites over the zucchini-tomato mixture. Cook until the egg bottom is set, about 5 minutes on the stove.

Place the frittata under the broiler about 4 inches from heat. Broil for 2 minutes. Sprinkle with the cheese and broil until the cheese melts.

Cut into 6 wedges and serve hot.

SERVES: 6 ═══════ **NUTRITIONAL INFORMATION PER SERVING** ═══════

Calories	56	Total Fat	1 g	Cholesterol	4 mg
Calories from Fat	19%	Saturated Fat	< 1 g	Sodium	102 mg

ITALIAN OMELET

To prevent the omelet from sticking to the pan, finish cooking under the broiler. The omelet will puff up and have a beautiful, colorful appearance.

4 egg whites
1 whole egg
1 tablespoon nonfat milk
non-stick cooking spray
1/4 cup fresh basil, chopped
   (or 2 teaspoons dried)
1/4 cup low-fat mozzarella
   cheese, shredded

4 ounces turkey-breast sausage,
   cooked and chopped*
3/4 cup nonfat marinara
   sauce, heated
Italian parsley
2 thick slices crusty Italian
   bread, toasted

Preheat broiler. Whip egg whites, egg and milk together. Spray a 9-inch broiler-safe pan with non-stick cooking spray. Heat to medium on stove. Pour eggs into pan. When they begin to set, sprinkle the omelet with basil, cheese and sausage. Place pan under broiler about 4 inches from heat. Broil until cheese melts and omelet puffs. Divide into two portions. Place on serving plates and top with marinara sauce.

Garnish with Italian parsley and serve with toasted crusty Italian bread.

*If turkey-breast sausage is not available in your area, brown 4 ounces ground turkey breast meat with 1/2 teaspoon dry oregano, 1/4 teaspoon black pepper and 1/4 teaspoon ground thyme.

SERVES: 2 ══════ **NUTRITIONAL INFORMATION PER SERVING** ══════

Calories	333	Total Fat	7 g	Cholesterol	154 mg
Calories from Fat	19%	Saturated Fat	4 g	Sodium	514 mg

VEGETABLE OMELET

This picture-perfect omelet is heavy on the vegetables and light on the cheese.

8 egg whites
1 tablespoon nonfat milk
non-stick cooking spray
2 cups mixed vegetables,
   such as steamed broccoli,
   mushrooms, tomatoes and onions

1/4 cup low-fat American
   cheese, shredded
chopped parsley for garnish

Preheat broiler. Whip egg whites and milk together. Spray a 9-inch broiler-safe pan with non-stick cooking spray. Heat to medium on the stove. Pour egg mixture into pan. When they begin to set, sprinkle the omelet with vegetables and cheese. Place pan under broiler about 4 inches from heat. Broil until cheese melts and omelet puffs.

Divide into two portions. Place on serving tray. Garnish with chopped parsley.

SERVES: 2 ===== **NUTRITIONAL INFORMATION PER SERVING** =====

Calories	249	Total Fat	5 g	Cholesterol	14 mg
Calories from Fat	19%	Saturated Fat	< 1 g	Sodium	321 mg

BROCCOLI CRABMEAT QUICHE

Replace traditional pastry crust with frozen Filo dough for a tender crust without much fat.

2 sheets Filo dough, defrosted
  and wrapped in damp towel
non-stick cooking spray
1 bunch broccoli, separated
  into flowerets
4 scallions, chopped
6 ounces crabmeat (fresh, frozen
  or canned and drained)

1/4 cup fresh parsley, chopped
1/4 cup provolone cheese, shredded
8 large egg whites
1 1/3 cups 1% buttermilk
1 teaspoon Dijon mustard
1/4 teaspoon paprika

Remove a sheet of Filo dough from damp towel. Double and place across 9-inch pie plate. Spray a little non-stick cooking spray between layers. Repeat with second sheet of Filo. Trim to fit. Bake unfilled crust at 375° F for 10 minutes. The crust will puff slightly.

Steam or microwave broccoli for 4 minutes, until it is bright green in color and is still crunchy. Drain. Mix broccoli with crabmeat, scallions and parsley. Distribute evenly over the Filo pastry and sprinkle with cheese. Whip egg whites with buttermilk, mustard and paprika. Pour over quiche.

Bake for 10 minutes at 375° F; reduce heat to 350° F and continue baking for 20 minutes longer. Let stand for 5 minutes before cutting. Cut into 8 wedges to serve.

For Vegetable Quiche: Add 1 cup broccoli, 1 cup steamed sweet peppers and 1 cup steamed, sliced mushrooms.

SERVES: 8 ═══════ **NUTRITIONAL INFORMATION PER SERVING** ═══════

Calories	92	Total Fat	2 g	Cholesterol	27 mg
Calories from Fat	17%	Saturated Fat	1 g	Sodium	345 mg

WHOLE-WHEAT CREPES

Here's a basic recipe for low-fat crepes, followed by two recipes for variations on crepe fillings. Make plenty of crepes, freeze or refrigerate, and you'll have a tasty supply of breakfasts on hand. You may fill these same crepes with fruit and yogurt for a great dessert!

1 cup whole-wheat or white flour	1/4 teaspoon salt
2/3 cup nonfat milk	3/4 cup water
6 large egg whites	non-stick cooking spray

Place flour, milk, egg whites, salt and water in a medium-sized bowl and mix thoroughly by hand or with an electric mixer. Refrigerate for 1 hour or overnight.

Spray a 5 or 6-inch non-stick crepe pan with a thick coating of non-stick cooking spray. Heat the pan over a medium hot burner. (If you are using an electric crepe pan, heat it to 375° F.) Pour 2 to 3 tablespoons crepe batter into the pan, tilting and swirling the hot pan as you add the batter. Use just enough batter to cover the bottom of the pan with a thick layer.

When the surface of the crepe is dry and the underside brown, turn the crepe. Allow other side to brown. This whole process will take about 5 minutes. Remove crepe and start a stack of crepes. Repeat with the remaining batter to make 12 crepes. As you stack the crepes, cover with plastic wrap.

Fill crepes and roll, or fill and fold edges in to form a square.

SERVES: 6 ═══════ **NUTRITIONAL INFORMATION PER SERVING** ═══════

Calories	94	Total Fat	< 1 g	Cholesterol	< 1 mg
Calories from Fat	4%	Saturated Fat	< 1 g	Sodium	159 mg

ASPARAGUS AND MUSHROOM CREPES

What could be more delightful than fresh vegetables, light cheeses and a sauce enhanced with wine. This recipe is a breakfast or brunch winner! It is high in calcium, fiber and flavor.

non-stick cooking spray
1/4 cup chicken stock
2 cups fresh or frozen asparagus,
   sliced in 1-inch pieces
1 cup fresh mushrooms, sliced
1/2 teaspoon lemon juice
1 teaspoon fresh tarragon
6 low-fat crepes (see recipe on page 52)
2 tablespoons low-fat Swiss
   cheese, shredded

3 tablespoons cornstarch
1 teaspoon Dijon mustard
1 1/2 cups plain nonfat yogurt
1/4 cup dry white wine
2 tablespoons grated Parmesan cheese
chopped chives, paprika and freshly
   ground black pepper for garnish
salt to taste

Preheat oven to 350° F. Spray a 9 x 9-inch baking dish with non-stick cooking spray. Place chicken stock in a non-stick frying pan. Add the asparagus and mushrooms and poach vegetables lightly for 5 minutes. Mix in the lemon juice and fresh tarragon. Place 1/4 cup asparagus mixture down the center of each crepe, fold and lay side-by-side, seam side down in the baking dish. Sprinkle with Swiss cheese.

Blend together cornstarch with Dijon mustard, yogurt, white wine and parmesan cheese. Spoon onto the crepes. Cover and bake 30 minutes or until the sauce is lightly browned.

Garnish with chopped chives, paprika and freshly ground black pepper. Serve immediately. Salt to taste.

SERVES: 6	NUTRITIONAL INFORMATION PER SERVING			
Calories	149	Total Fat	3 g	Cholesterol	8 mg
Calories from Fat	16%	Saturated Fat	1 g	Sodium	224 mg

MEXI-CHICKEN CREPES

A south-of-the-border taste rolled in a crepe. This easy-to-make recipe is very low in calories and has a wonderful flavor. It is even better reheated the second day!

3 large, ripe tomatoes, chopped
1 tablespoon green chilies or
  Jalapeño peppers, chopped
1/2 cup fresh cilantro, chopped
non-stick cooking spray
6 low-fat crepes (see recipe on page 52)
1 1/2 cups cooked chicken breast,
  cut into bite-size pieces

1/4 cup low-fat Monterey Jack
  cheese, shredded
1/2 cup low-fat sour cream
  (see recipe on page 24)
3 green onions, chopped
sprigs of cilantro
salt and freshly ground pepper to taste

Preheat the oven to 375° F.

Place the chopped tomatoes with chilies or Jalapeños and cilantro in a blender. Pulse several times with an on-off motion until salsa is chunky.

Spray a 9 x 9-inch baking dish with non-stick cooking spray. Spread half of the salsa mixture on the bottom of the baking dish.

Place 1/4 cup of the chicken down the middle of each crepe and roll. Place seam side down in the baking dish on top of salsa. Spoon remaining salsa over crepes. Sprinkle with cheese. Cover and bake for 25 minutes. Filling will be hot and cheese melted.

Spoon the sour cream down the centers of the crepes. Sprinkle with green onions. Garnish with sprigs of cilantro. Salt and pepper to taste. Serve immediately.

Quick and Easy: Use 3 cups of a good prepared salsa to replace first 3 ingredients.

SERVES: 6 ═══════════ **NUTRITIONAL INFORMATION PER SERVING** ═══════

Calories	217	Total Fat	< 3 g	Cholesterol	51 mg
Calories from Fat	12%	Saturated Fat	1 g	Sodium	224 mg

SUNSHINE-STYLE FRENCH TOAST

Using orange juice to replace egg yolks is a great way to add a tangy flavor, a golden color and to help brown the bread.

1/2 cup nonfat milk
6 egg whites
2 tablespoons sugar
1/2 cup orange juice
1 teaspoon orange peel, grated

8 1/2-inch-thick slices day-old French
   bread or wheat bread
non-stick cooking spray
1/4 cup powdered sugar
1/2 cup maple syrup

In medium-sized mixing bowl, beat milk, egg whites, sugar, orange juice and orange peel until the mixture is thick, blended and smooth. Pour the mixture into a shallow bowl.

Dip the bread slices into the egg mixture and allow to rest on a large jelly roll pan. Make sure all of the egg mixture is utilized on the 8 bread slices.

Spray a large griddle or a large skillet with non-stick cooking spray.

Heat to medium hot (about 325° F). Without crowding, brown the toast slices on both sides. Allow at least 5 minutes per slice to insure cooking throughout.

Dust with the powdered sugar. Serve 2 pieces of french toast on each of 4 plates. Top with hot maple syrup or *Fruit Sauce* (see recipe on page 43).

SERVES: 4 ══════ **NUTRITIONAL INFORMATION PER SERVING** ══════

Calories	299	Total Fat	1.5 g	Cholesterol	< 1 mg
Calories from Fat	5%	Saturated Fat	< 1 g	Sodium	315 mg

Soups & Stews

Soups and stews are great dishes with which to experiment. Use your creativity by adding extras like herbs, cayenne pepper or crunchy toppings. As starters, side dishes or main courses, soups and stews hit the spot in summer as well as winter.

About Making Stock...

It's always preferable to make vegetable and meat stocks from scratch – they taste fresher, they are more flavorful and they are not loaded with salt as are most prepared stocks.

However, when you're in a pinch for time, don't hesitate to use a prepared stock. When purchasing a prepared stock, look at the ingredient list carefully and select the stock with the least fat; some stocks, even bouillon cubes, are laden with fat.

HOMEMADE STOCK

The base for so many soups, this recipe can be made with or without meat.

bouquet garni (Fill a cheesecloth with
   6 peppercorns, fresh sprigs of thyme,
   basil leaves, parsley and other herbs;
   then tie it and smash it with the side
   of a cleaver to release volatile oils of
   herbs and to crush peppercorns)
3 quarts water
3 cups onion, chopped
2 cloves garlic, smashed
2 cups carrot, cut into chunks
2 cups celery tops with leaves
2 cups mushrooms
2 cups zucchini, cut into chunks
3 bay leaves
3 pounds meat, poultry
   or fish bones (optional)

Place all ingredients in a large soup
kettle or pressure cooker. Simmer for
3 hours or pressure cook for 30
minutes. Remove bouquet garni,
strain stock and season to taste.
Recipe makes 3 quarts.

SERVES: 12 ══════ **NUTRITIONAL INFORMATION PER SERVING** ═══════

Calories	14	Total Fat	< 1 g	Cholesterol	0 mg
Calories from Fat	8%	Saturated Fat	< 1 g	Sodium	6 mg

GAZPACHO

Gazpacho is the perfect way to enjoy summer garden vegetables. Serve as a first course with crusty bread or with a turkey breast sandwich for lunch (see color photo on page 61).

3 large tomatoes, peeled and diced
1 green pepper, seeded and chopped
1 yellow pepper, seeded and chopped
6 scallions, sliced and chopped
1 large cucumber, peeled and chopped
1/2 cup pimiento, chopped

1/3 cup balsamic vinegar
3 cups tomato or vegetable juice
2 cloves garlic, crushed
1/4 cup cilantro, finely chopped
few drops hot pepper sauce (optional)
salt and pepper to taste

Process 2 of the tomatoes in blender until chunky smooth. Add to remaining ingredients. Refrigerate for at least 2 hours, season with salt and pepper, garnish and serve.

SERVES: 6	NUTRITIONAL INFORMATION PER SERVING				
Calories	67	Total Fat	< 1 g	Cholesterol	0 mg
Calories from Fat	6%	Saturated Fat	< 1 g	Sodium	25 mg

WHITE GAZPACHO

3 cucumbers, peeled
1 clove garlic
3 cups chicken stock
   (homemade or prepared)
3 cups low-fat yogurt

2 tablespoons white vinegar
salt and pepper to taste
1/2 cup scallions, sliced
1/2 cup cilantro, chopped
2 tomatoes, chopped

Cut cucumbers into pieces and process in blender with garlic and 1 cup chicken stock. Combine with remaining stock yogurt and vinegar, and salt and pepper to taste. Ladle into chilled bowls and top with scallions, cilantro and chopped tomatoes.

SERVES: 6	NUTRITIONAL INFORMATION PER SERVING				
Calories	113	Total Fat	2 g	Cholesterol	7 mg
Calories from Fat	17%	Saturated Fat	1 g	Sodium	90 mg

SPLIT PEA SOUP

This smooth favorite sticks to your ribs but doesn't have loads of fat. It is, however, loaded with fiber.

12 ounces split green peas
1 quart water
1 medium onion, chopped
2 carrots, cut into 2-inch pieces
2 ribs celery, cut into 2-inch pieces
2 parsley sprigs
1 clove garlic
1/2 teaspoon sugar

1/8 teaspoon thyme
4 cups chicken stock
  (homemade or prepared)
8 ounces Canadian bacon,
  slivered in 1/4 x 1-inch pieces
fresh parsley, chopped
salt and pepper to taste

In a large soup pot, combine the peas with 1 quart water. Bring the mixture to a boil, reduce heat, cover and simmer for 45 minutes. Watch split peas carefully so that they do not boil over. Add the onion, carrots, celery, parsley, garlic, sugar, thyme and chicken stock. Cover and simmer for 1 hour. Cool slightly.

In a food processor or in a blender, purée soup. This should be done in 3 or 4 batches. Return the pea purée to soup pot, heat and garnish with slivered Canadian bacon and chopped parsley. Salt and pepper to taste.

SERVES: 8 ═══ **NUTRITIONAL INFORMATION PER SERVING** ═══

| Calories | 135 | Total Fat | 3 g | Cholesterol | 16 mg |
| Calories from Fat | 19% | Saturated Fat | < 1 g | Sodium | 451 mg |

BEEF STEW WITH BARLEY

This stew is a hearty meal in a bowl, with chunks of lean beef, vegetables and tender barley. Serve with Minted Citrus Salad (see page 94) or with a tossed vegetable salad.

non-stick cooking spray
1 pound beef stew meat,
   trimmed of all fat
4 cups beef stock
   (homemade or prepared)

1 cup pearl onions (fresh or canned)
1 teaspoon dry basil leaves
1/4 cup fresh parsley, chopped
1 1/2 cups barley, uncooked
1 1/2 cups carrots, sliced
salt and freshly ground pepper to taste

Spray a Dutch oven with nonfat cooking spray. Heat to hot. Add beef and brown on all sides. Remove beef to paper towels and pat off excess fat. Rinse Dutch oven. In the Dutch oven, blend together browned beef, beef stock, onions, basil, parsley, barley and carrots. Bring to a boil, cover and reduce heat to simmer. Simmer for 1 hour. Salt and pepper to taste. Ladle stew into wide bowls and serve immediately.

SERVES: 6   **NUTRITIONAL INFORMATION PER SERVING**

Calories	346	Total Fat	6 g	Cholesterol	54 mg
Calories from Fat	16%	Saturated Fat	2 g	Sodium	60 mg

VICHYSSOISE

3 cups chicken or vegetable stock
   (homemade or prepared)
1/2 leek bulb, sliced
3 celery ribs with tops, sliced
2 large red-skin potatoes,
   cubed with skins

1 cup evaporated skim milk
1/4 teaspoon white pepper
1/4 teaspoon hot sauce
chopped parsley
salt and freshly ground pepper to taste

In a large soup pot, heat the stock with the leek, celery and potatoes. When the mixture boils, reduce heat, cover and simmer for 30 minutes.

The potatoes will be very tender. Add the milk, pepper and hot sauce. Salt to taste. Chill for at least 4 hours before serving.

To Serve: Place in chilled bowls. Top with ground pepper and chopped parsley.

SERVES: 8 ══════════ **NUTRITIONAL INFORMATION PER SERVING** ══════════

Calories	74	Total Fat	< 1 g	Cholesterol	1 mg
Calories from Fat	2%	Saturated Fat	< 1 g	Sodium	56 mg

BLACK BEAN STEW

1 12-ounce package black beans, washed and picked over
non-stick cooking spray
1 1/2 cups green onion with tops, chopped
3 cloves garlic, minced
1 26-ounce can tomatoes
1 cup fresh or canned pumpkin purée (not pumpkin pie filling!)
1 1/2 cups beef stock (homemade or prepared)

1 tablespoon cumin
1 1/2 tablespoons balsamic or red wine vinegar
8 ounces Canadian bacon, cut into small squares
1 cup dry sherry
1 cup Yogurt Cheese (see recipe on page 24)
sliced green onion for garnish
10 lime slices

Place the beans in a large saucepan and cover with boiling water to a level of 3 inches above the beans. Simmer until the beans are tender, about 3 hours. Drain. Spray large saucepan thoroughly with non-stick cooking spray. Sauté onion and garlic until just soft. Add tomatoes, pumpkin purée, beef stock, cumin, vinegar and black beans. Simmer for 25 minutes. Add bacon, black pepper and sherry and heat thoroughly. Salt to taste. Serve in large bowls with a dollop of yogurt cheese, a sprinkle of green onions and a slice of lime.

Quick and Easy: Use 1 19-ounce can black beans (frijoles negros), drained, in place of the dry beans.

SERVES: 10 ══════════ **NUTRITIONAL INFORMATION PER SERVING** ══════════

Calories	154	Total Fat	3 g	Cholesterol	15 mg
Calories from Fat	16%	Saturated Fat	< 1 g	Sodium	490 mg

CLAM CHOWDER

The ultimate in clam chowders – it is rich and delectable but has only 11% calories from fat!

6 dozen fresh clams, scrubbed
　(or 12-ounce can of chopped clams)
1 cup onion, chopped
3 tablespoons fresh thyme
3 bay leaves
1 cup dry white wine
3 cups chicken stock
3 cups potatoes, peeled and diced
1 cup leeks, sliced
1 10-ounce package frozen corn

3 tablespoons cornstarch
1/2 cup water
1 cup Yogurt Cheese
　(see recipe on page 24)
4 ounces Canadian bacon, chopped
　into small pieces
sprigs of thyme for garnish

If you are using fresh clams, soak in cold water with a little cornmeal for 1 hour. Scrub shells of all sand.

In a large stock pot, poach onion, thyme and bay leaves in white wine. Add chicken stock and heat to boil. Steam clams in boiling stock just until they open, about 5 minutes. Remove clams from water; cool and remove their meat. If stock is at all sandy, strain through a very fine strainer or through several layers of cheesecloth.

Add potatoes and leeks to stock and cook until tender, about 20 minutes. Add corn and continue cooking for 10 minutes. Blend cornstarch with yogurt cheese and 1/2 cup water and add it to the stock pot, gradually, whisking for a smooth sauce. Reheat with Canadian bacon and clams.

To Serve: Pour hot chowder into serving bowls and garnish with sprigs of thyme.

SERVES: 6 ━━━━━━ **NUTRITIONAL INFORMATION PER SERVING** ━━━━━━

Calories	272	Total Fat	3 g	Cholesterol	42 mg
Calories from Fat	11%	Saturated Fat	1 g	Sodium	383 mg

VEGETABLE CHOWDER

This thick chowder is chock full of six different vegetables and also makes a great stock. If it is puréed in the blender, it can be a base for hearty bean and pasta soups such as Golden Lentil Soup with Potatoes (see recipe on page 70).

1 teaspoon olive oil
3 large onions, chopped
3 cloves garlic, minced
1 cup fresh or frozen corn
1 cup carrots, sliced
1 cup fresh or frozen green beans

1 cup zucchini, sliced
1 cup tomato, chopped
1 cup fresh mushrooms, sliced
12 cups water
salt and pepper to taste

Heat olive oil in a large stock pot. Add onion and garlic and cook until well browned. Add remaining vegetables and 12 cups of water. Heat to boiling, cover and then reduce heat to a simmer. Simmer for 3 hours, adding more water as necessary. Salt and pepper to taste. Cool stock. Serve as is or purée in 3 or 4 batches in a blender or a food processor.

SERVES: 12		NUTRITIONAL INFORMATION PER SERVING			
Calories	47	Total Fat	< 1 g	Cholesterol	0 mg
Calories from Fat	11%	Saturated Fat	< 1 g	Sodium	10 mg

MEATLESS CHILI SOUP

1 14-ounce can kidney beans
2 cups salsa (see recipe on page 38)

1 cup frozen corn

Blend all ingredients in a medium-sized saucepan. Heat to a boil, reduce heat, cover and cook 6 to 10 minutes, until corn kernels are heated through.

SERVES: 4		NUTRITIONAL INFORMATION PER SERVING			
Calories	136	Total Fat	< 1 g	Cholesterol	0 mg
Calories from Fat	4%	Saturated Fat	< 1 g	Sodium	332 mg

ITALIAN SOUP

For a real Italian meal in a single bowl, try this tempting dish that incorporates low-fat Italian turkey-breast sausage, tomato sauce, tortellini and Italian spices.

5 cups beef stock
  (homemade or prepared)
1 cup dry red wine
1 pound low-fat,
  Italian turkey-breast link sausage
1 cup onion, chopped
2 cloves garlic, minced
1 cup carrots, sliced
1 cup celery, chopped
1 green pepper, chopped

2 cups chopped tomatoes
  (or 16 ounces canned)
8 ounces tomato sauce
1 teaspoon fresh oregano
several sprigs thyme
8 ounces frozen or fresh tortellini
freshly chopped basil and parsley
  for garnish
1/4 cup grated parmesan cheese
  for garnish

In a stock pot, heat stock and wine. Add sausage and simmer for 10 minutes until sausage is cooked. Remove sausage. Add onion, garlic, carrots, celery, green pepper, tomatoes, tomato sauce, oregano and thyme. Cook until vegetables are tender, about 30 minutes. Slice sausage into thin rounds and add to the stock with tortellini. Cook an additional 20 minutes or until tortellini are cooked.

To Serve: Ladle into serving bowls and garnish with basil, parsley and a little cheese.

Quick and Easy: Use frozen packages of chopped onion, carrot, celery and green pepper.

SERVES: 8 ══════ **NUTRITIONAL INFORMATION PER SERVING** ══════

Calories	250	Total Fat	4 g	Cholesterol	50 mg
Calories from Fat	13%	Saturated Fat	< 1 g	Sodium	637 mg

JAMBALAYA

This wonderful Creole-inspired stew gets intense flavor from the ham hock and the exciting blend of fresh thyme, peppercorns, clove and cayenne pepper.

1 smoked ham hock (1 to 1 1/2 pounds)
1 onion, chopped
1 teaspoon olive oil
1/2 cup celery, chopped
2 cloves garlic, minced
2 tablespoons unsalted tomato paste
1 bunch fresh thyme
  (or 2 tablespoons dry)
8 cloves
12 peppercorns

1 teaspoon cayenne pepper
2 pints water
1 3/4 pounds fresh green shrimp,
  unpeeled and uncooked
1 1/2 cups rice, cooked
2 cups dry white wine
8 ounces Canadian bacon, cubed
1 teaspoon fresh thyme, chopped
  (or 1/2 teaspoon dry)
2 tablespoons parsley, chopped

Cook ham hock in 3 cups water for 3 hours. Discard hock, strain, chill and defat the stock. Reserve stock in a large saucepan.

In a large stock pot, sauté onion in oil. Add celery and garlic and cook until brown and soft. Add tomato paste and sauté until it reaches a deep brown color. Add ham stock to this mixture. Process the bunch of fresh thyme, cloves, peppercorns and cayenne in a blender or coffee mill. Put the mixture into the stock pot.

In a large saucepan, heat 2 pints water to boiling. Add shrimp and allow to boil for 3 minutes. Remove shrimp to ice water. Peel shrimp.

Add rice, wine, Canadian bacon, shrimp, one teaspoon fresh thyme and parsley into the stock pot. Heat, ladle into bowls and serve immediately.

SERVES: 6	NUTRITIONAL INFORMATION PER SERVING				
Calories	307	Total Fat	5 g	Cholesterol	170 mg
Calories from Fat	15%	Saturated Fat	2 g	Sodium	593 mg

GOLDEN LENTIL SOUP WITH POTATOES

This soup is so easy to prepare and it's packed with flavor and good nutrition.

12 ounces golden lentils,
   picked over and cleaned
8 cups beef stock
   (homemade or prepared)
1 16-ounce can tomatoes,
   chopped with liquid
2 tablespoons parsley, chopped
1 large onion, diced

1 bay leaf
2 cloves garlic, crushed
2 medium carrots, thinly sliced
4 medium red potatoes,
   cubed with skins
salt and pepper to taste
chopped tomato for garnish
parsley sprigs for garnish

In a large soup pot, combine lentils with beef stock, tomatoes, parsley, onion, bay leaf and garlic. Bring to a boil, reduce heat, cover and simmer for 1 hour until lentils are tender. Add carrots and potato and more water as necessary to maintain the same level of liquid.

Cook for an additional 30 minutes, stirring occasionally until potatoes are tender. Salt and pepper to taste. Remove bay leaf before serving.

To Serve: Ladle into serving bowls. Top each bowl with chopped tomato and a large sprig of parsley.

SERVES: 12 ═══════ **NUTRITIONAL INFORMATION PER SERVING** ═══════

Calories	120	Total Fat	< 1 g	Cholesterol	0 mg
Calories from Fat	3%	Saturated Fat	< 1 g	Sodium	74 mg

TORTILLA SOUP

A crunchy soup with a nice spicy flavor. Use any or all of the 5 toppings.

1 teaspoon olive oil
1 small onion, chopped
8 ounces tomato sauce
4 cups chicken stock
  (homemade or prepared)
8 ounces lean pork tenderloin, ground
1 clove garlic, crushed
1 Jalapeño pepper, minced
1/2 teaspoon each chili powder,
  cumin, paprika
4 ounces chilies, chopped

Toppings
4 corn tortillas, cut into 1-inch strips
1/2 cup fresh cilantro, chopped
1 large tomato, diced
1/2 cup scallions, chopped
1/2 cup cucumber, chopped

Preheat oven to 350° F.

In a large stock pot, heat olive oil. Add onions and sauté until translucent. Add tomato sauce and reduce until the sauce starts to caramelize on the bottom of the pan. Add chicken stock, stirring in the cooked bits from the bottom of the pan. Add ground tenderloin, garlic, Jalapeño pepper, spices and chilies and simmer for 20 minutes to cook sausage.

Place tortillas on an ungreased cookie sheet and bake until crisp, about 5 to 7 minutes.

To Serve: Ladle soup into large, heated bowls, adding tortilla strips, cilantro, tomato, scallions and cucumber toppings.

Quick and Easy: Use baked tortilla chips for crisp tortillas. Use prepared salsa for chopped topping.

SERVES: 4		NUTRITIONAL INFORMATION PER SERVING			
Calories	222	Total Fat	5 g	Cholesterol	53 mg
Calories from Fat	20%	Saturated Fat	1 g	Sodium	469 mg

Breads, Rolls & Muffins

There's nothing quite like the smell of fresh baked bread coming from your own kitchen. Breadmaking is a gratifying activity, whether you do it by hand, with your electric mixer or food processor, or with your bread machine. Here are some all-time favorite bread recipes as well as a few new ones to try.

BAGELS

Bagels take a little time and skill, and are definitely worth the effort. You'll love the soft, moist texture and the crisp outer crust! This recipe is very low in fat.

non-stick cooking spray
1 1/2 cups whole-wheat flour
1 package (1/4-ounce) active dry yeast
2 to 2 1/2 cups all-purpose
　white flour, divided

1 1/2 cups very warm water (115° F)
3 tablespoons granulated sugar
1 tablespoon salt
1 gallon water
1/2 cup seedless raisins

Spray a large baking sheet with a thick coating of non-stick cooking spray. Blend whole-wheat flour with yeast and 1 1/2 cups white flour. Combine the warm water, sugar and salt and pour over the flour mixture.

Beat with an electric mixer or with a food processor fitted with dough hook for 1/2 minute. Blend in the remaining flour and knead until the dough is smooth and satiny, 4 minutes with electric dough hook; 10 minutes by hand. Add raisins.

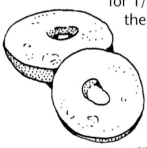

Spray a medium-sized bowl with non-stick cooking spray. Place dough in bowl, cover and allow to rise in a warm, draft-free place for 10 minutes. Divide the dough into 12 portions and shape each portion into a smooth ball. Gently shape a 1-inch hole in the center of each ball. Place bagels on the prepared baking sheet. Cover and allow to rise in a warm, draft-free place for 20 minutes. Preheat the oven to broil.

Broil the bagels for 5 minutes, 4 inches from the source of heat. Turn the bagels once, but do not allow them to brown.

Reduce the oven temperature to 375° F. Heat 1 gallon of water to boiling. Cook the bagels in boiling water, 4 to 5 at a time, for 7 minutes, turning once. Drain.

Place the hot bagels on a greased baking sheet. Bake in a 375° F oven for 25 to 30 minutes until bagels are deep brown with a crisp outer crust.

Freeze any bagels not eaten in 2 days. To reheat, defrost, split and toast the bagels in an electric toaster. Or, rinse with water and refresh for a few minutes in a 350° F oven.

SERVES: 12 ══════ **NUTRITIONAL INFORMATION PER SERVING** ══════

Calories	158	Total Fat	< 1 g	Cholesterol	0 mg
Calories from Fat	3%	Saturated Fat	0 g	Sodium	180 mg

CHEESE GARLIC BREAD

Broil leftover slices for a delicious, low-fat garlic toast.

1 package (1/4 ounce) active dry yeast
3/4 cup warm water (115° F)
2 tablespoons onion, grated
2 cloves garlic, crushed
1 teaspoon oil
1 1/2 cups all-purpose flour

1/2 cup bread flour
1 teaspoon salt
1/4 cup finely chopped basil,
    Italian parsley or curly parsley
1/4 cup parmesan cheese, grated

Allow yeast to soak in warm water for 5 minutes. In a small frying pan, sauté onion and garlic in oil until well browned.

Blend flour with salt. Add yeast mixture, onion and garlic mixture, herbs and cheese. Knead until the dough is smooth and satiny, about 10 minutes by hand, 5 minutes by machine. Place in a greased bowl and top with a warm, wet towel. Allow to rise in a warm place for 30 minutes.

Place dough on a well-floured surface and knead down. Roll out to an 8 x 9-inch rectangle. Roll both long edges into the center to form a loaf. Place on a greased baking sheet and allow to rise in a warm place a second time for 30 minutes. Preheat oven to 375° F. Place bread in oven. Toss 3 to 4 ice cubes into the oven to give the bread a crisp crust. Bake 20 to 25 minutes, until bread is well browned.

SERVES: 12 ══════ **NUTRITIONAL INFORMATION PER SERVING** ══════

Calories	89	Total Fat	1 g	Cholesterol	2 mg
Calories from Fat	12%	Saturated Fat	< 1 g	Sodium	217 mg

BANANA CINNAMON SWIRLS

These breakfast rolls are scrumptious even without the glaze.

2 packages (1/4 ounce each)
  active dry yeast
1/2 cup very warm water
1 cup nonfat milk
1/4 cup plus 1 tablespoon light
  margarine, divided
1/4 cup sugar
1/2 cup low-fat sour cream
  (see recipe on page 24)
1 teaspoon salt
1 cup hot oat bran cereal

1 egg
1 banana, mashed
4 1/2 to 5 cups flour
1/2 cup brown sugar
1 teaspoon cinnamon
2 tablespoons almonds, sliced

Glaze
1 cup confectioners' sugar
7 teaspoons milk
1/4 teaspoon almond extract

Add yeast to warm water and allow to stand 10 minutes. Combine milk and 1/4 cup margarine and heat to warm. Pour milk into a large mixing bowl and add sugar, sour cream, salt and oat bran. Allow to stand for 5 minutes to soften the oat bran.

Add egg, banana and yeast. Mix well. Blend in flour to form a soft dough. Turn onto a lightly-floured surface and knead until smooth, about 10 minutes. Put dough into an oiled bowl, cover with a damp cloth and allow to rise in a warm place for 1 hour. Combine brown sugar, cinnamon and sliced almonds.

Knead down dough and turn it onto a lightly-floured surface. Divide in half and allow to rest for 10 minutes. Roll out the dough into two 15 x 10-inch rectangles.

Brush with remaining tablespoon of margarine and sprinkle with brown sugar mixture. Roll in jelly roll style, beginning with a long side. Seal edges. Repeat with remaining dough. Cut each roll into 18 1-inch slices and place, cut side down, onto greased baking pans. Cover and allow to rise for 45 minutes.

Preheat oven to 375° F. Bake 16 minutes or until rolls are golden. When the rolls have cooled, glaze with 1 cup confectioners' sugar blended with 7 teaspoons milk and 1/4 teaspoon almond extract, if desired.

Quick and Easy: You may halve the recipe and mix the first 11 ingredients in a bread machine. Then roll out as directed in the recipe.

SERVES: 36　　**NUTRITIONAL INFORMATION PER SERVING**

| Calories | 97 | Total Fat | 2 g | Cholesterol | 6 mg |
| Calories from Fat | 19% | Saturated Fat | < 1 g | Sodium | 87 mg |

HOT CROSS BUNS

Here's a simple, yet foolproof recipe for a traditional holiday treat that is so easy you can make it all year round.

1 1/2 cups all-purpose flour, divided
1 1/2 cups whole-wheat flour, divided
1 package (1/4 ounce) active dry yeast
1/4 cup sugar
3/4 teaspoon salt
1/4 teaspoon nutmeg
1/4 teaspoon cinnamon
1 cup 1% buttermilk
2 tablespoons light margarine

1 egg, beaten
1/3 cup currants
non-stick cooking spray
1 egg white, beaten

Icing
1 cup confectioners' sugar
2 teaspoons hot nonfat milk

In a mixing bowl or a food processor bowl, blend 1 1/4 cups of the white flour, 1 1/4 cups of the whole-wheat flour, the yeast, sugar, salt, nutmeg and cinnamon. Heat the buttermilk to almost boiling. Add the margarine and stir until it melts. Pour the buttermilk mixture into the flour mixture and blend with a wooden spoon or with dough hooks. Add the egg and the currants and knead in enough of the remaining flour to make a dough that is smooth and satiny (about 10 minutes by hand or 5 minutes with a mixer or food processor).

Preheat oven to 425° F. Spray a medium-sized bowl with non-stick cooking spray. Place the dough in the bowl, cover and allow dough to rise in a warm, draft-free place for 20 minutes. Spray a 10-inch square baking pan with non-stick cooking spray.

Place the dough on a cutting board and cut into 16 parts. Form into 16 smooth balls and place in the baking pan. Cover and allow dough to rise in a warm, draft-free place for 15 minutes. Brush the tops with the egg white.

Bake the Hot Cross Buns 12 to 15 minutes until evenly browned. Cool the buns in the pan.

To make icing, blend confectioners' sugar and hot milk into a smooth paste. With the icing, make a cross on top of each cooled Hot Cross Bun.

SERVES: 16		NUTRITIONAL INFORMATION PER SERVING			
Calories	144	Total Fat	1 g	Cholesterol	14 mg
Calories from Fat	9%	Saturated Fat	< 1 g	Sodium	141 mg

FOCACCIA (GOURMET PIZZA)

You'll see a lot of variations of focaccia. This one is light, crusty and flavorful.

1 package (1/4 ounce) active dry yeast
3/4 cup very warm water, divided
2 1/2 to 3 cups flour, divided
1 teaspoon olive oil

1/4 cup parmesan cheese, grated
1/4 cup basil, chopped
1 teaspoon salt

Soak yeast in 1/2 cup warm water for 5 minutes. Add 1 1/4 cups flour and knead for 5 minutes until flour is well blended. Allow to rest in a warm place for 15 minutes.

Knead down dough and add remaining water, olive oil, cheese, basil, salt and remaining flour as needed to make a workable dough. Mix well, then knead dough to a smooth, elastic consistency.

Roll focaccia to fit a 10-inch pizza pan. Bake at 400° F for 25 minutes.

Cut into 8 wedges and serve immediately.

SERVES: 8		NUTRITIONAL INFORMATION PER SERVING			
Calories	153	Total Fat	2 g	Cholesterol	2 mg
Calories from Fat	11%	Saturated Fat	< 1 g	Sodium	326 mg

ITALIAN BREAD • BAGUETTES • CRUSTY ITALIAN ROLLS

A very practical and versatile recipe that makes Italian bread, baguettes, crusty hard rolls, pizza crust and more. Add herbs, work with different grains such as cornmeal and just have fun with this recipe.

1 package (1/4 ounce) active dry yeast
2 cups very warm water (115° F)
2 cups all-purpose flour
1 cup whole-wheat flour

1 cup bread flour
1 teaspoon salt
non-stick cooking spray

Mix yeast with warm water in a small bowl. Set aside for 5 minutes. Meanwhile, blend the three flours and salt in a large bowl. Make a well in the middle and add yeast mixture. Knead by hand for 10 minutes or with a mixer or bread machine for 5 minutes or until dough is smooth and satiny.

Spray a warm bowl with non-stick cooking spray. Place dough in bowl, cover dough and allow dough to rise in a draft-free place for 30 minutes. Remove to a floured board and allow to rest 10 minutes.

For Italian Bread: Divide into 2 pieces. Form into 2 large loaves and place on an oiled baking sheet. Allow to rise for 1 hour. Preheat oven to 425° F. Bake Italian bread loaves for 20 to 25 minutes. For a crisp crust, throw several ice cubes onto the oven floor halfway through the baking cycle. Six slices per loaf, one slice per serving.

For Baguettes: Divide into 4 pieces. With a rolling pin, roll to a length of 14 inches. Turn edges under, forming a long, slender baguette and place on an oiled baking sheet. Allow to rise for 1 hour. Preheat oven to 425° F. Bake baguettes for 15 minutes. For a crisp crust, throw several ice cubes onto the oven floor halfway through the baking cycle. Three slices per baguette, one slice per serving.

For Hard Rolls: Form into 12 balls. Place on prepared baking pan. Allow to rise a second time for 1 hour. Preheat oven to 425° F for 10 minutes. For a crisp crust, throw several ice cubes onto the oven floor halfway through the baking cycle. One roll per serving.

SERVES: 12	NUTRITIONAL INFORMATION PER SERVING				
Calories	160	Total Fat	< 1 g	Cholesterol	0 mg
Calories from Fat	4%	Saturated Fat	< 1 g	Sodium	179 mg

PIZZA DOUGH

Create your own toppings for this pizza. The crust is easy to make and freezes well before or after baking.

1 package (1/4 ounce) active dry yeast
3/4 cup very warm water
2 cups flour

1 teaspoon salt
1 teaspoon sugar

Soak yeast in water for 5 minutes. Add flour, salt and sugar and mix to blend. Knead for 2 to 3 minutes until flour is well blended. Allow to rest in a warm place for 15 minutes. Preheat oven to 450° F. Divide pizza dough into 2 portions. Roll each to fit 10-inch pizza pan.

Top with low-fat toppings such as vegetables (red and green peppers, basil leaves, mushrooms, asparagus tips), low-fat cheese (cottage or mozzarella) and tomato sauce. Bake 12 to 14 minutes until bottom of crust is deep brown.

SERVES: 6	NUTRITIONAL INFORMATION PER SERVING				
Calories	146	Total Fat	< 1 g	Cholesterol	0 mg
Calories from Fat	2%	Saturated Fat	< 1 g	Sodium	356 mg

SCONES

These yummy scones are popular with children as well as adults.

3 cups all-purpose flour
1/2 cup currants
2 tablespoons granulated sugar
3 teaspoons baking powder
1/2 teaspoon salt
1/2 teaspoon baking soda
1/2 cup low-fat yogurt

12 tablespoons oil
2 large egg whites
2 tablespoons nonfat milk
  for brushing tops of scones
1 tablespoon granulated sugar
  for sprinkling tops of scones

Preheat oven to 400° F.

In a large bowl, combine flour with the currants, sugar, baking powder, salt, soda, yogurt, oil and egg whites. Blend until the mixture holds together well.

Place mixture on a pastry board that has been sprinkled lightly with flour. Knead dough lightly, about 1 minute. Divide the dough into 12 portions (or 24 smaller portions to make mini scones). Smooth each portion into a 2-inch circle with a slightly rounded top. Brush the tops with milk and sprinkle with sugar.

Place the scones, 2 inches apart, on an ungreased baking sheet. Bake 12 minutes for mini scones or 15 minutes for regular scones or until scones are golden brown. Serve hot.

SERVES: 12 ═══════════ **NUTRITIONAL INFORMATION PER SERVING** ═══════════

Calories	164	Total Fat	3 g	Cholesterol	< 1 mg
Calories from Fat	15%	Saturated Fat	< 1 g	Sodium	224 mg

CORN BREAD

A corn bread with a chewy texture that's perfect for dipping into soups and stews.

1 tablespoon oil
1 cup cornmeal (white or yellow)
1 cup flour
2 teaspoons baking powder
1/2 teaspoon baking soda

1 teaspoon salt
1 tablespoon honey
1 tablespoon wheat germ
1 egg white, lightly beaten
1 cup 1% buttermilk

Preheat oven to 400° F. Pour oil into a 9 x 5 x 3-inch bread pan or into a 9-inch round or square cast iron skillet. Place the pan or the skillet into a hot oven and allow it to heat.

Mix the cornmeal with the flour, baking powder, baking soda and salt. Add the honey, wheat germ, egg white and buttermilk. Stir the mixture until it is just blended. The batter will be thick.

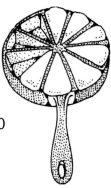

Carefully pour cornmeal mixture into hot pan. Bake 15 to 20 minutes or until browned. Remove pan from the oven, cut cornbread into 8 servings and serve immediately.

SERVES: 8 ══════════ **NUTRITIONAL INFORMATION PER SERVING** ══════

Calories	154	Total Fat	3 g	Cholesterol	27 mg
Calories from Fat	19%	Saturated Fat	< 1 g	Sodium	492 mg

BLUEBERRY MUFFINS

From mixing bowl to serving platter in 25 minutes! These easy-to-make muffins are a low-fat favorite.

non-stick cooking spray
2 8-ounce cups blueberry-flavored
  yogurt (1.5% milk fat)
1 teaspoon baking powder
3 large egg whites

1/4 cup granulated sugar
1 tablespoon oil
1/2 cup water
2 cups all-purpose flour

Preheat the oven to 400° F. Spray 2 6-cup muffin tins with non-stick cooking spray.

In a medium-sized mixing bowl, blend the blueberry yogurt with the baking powder. Allow this mixture to sit for 5 minutes or until the mixture becomes bubbly. Blend the egg whites, sugar, oil and water into the yogurt mixture. Fold the flour into this mixture until just moistened.

Divide into the muffin tins. Bake 20 minutes or until the muffins are lightly browned and firm to the touch. Remove the muffins from the tins immediately.

Muffins may be stored in the refrigerator for up to 3 weeks or in the freezer for 3 months. To reheat, microwave each muffin on high for 30 seconds or heat in a 350° F oven for 10 minutes.

SERVES: 12	NUTRITIONAL INFORMATION PER SERVING				
Calories	138	Total Fat	2 g	Cholesterol	2 mg
Calories from Fat	11%	Saturated Fat	< 1 g	Sodium	64 mg

CARROT GINGER MUFFINS

This tasty muffin will remind you of a moist carrot cake. For sensational flavor, use freshly grated ginger root.

non-stick cooking spray
1 teaspoon baking powder
1 cup 1% buttermilk
1/4 cup corn syrup
1/2 cup brown sugar, firmly packed
1/2 cup raisins
3 cups grated carrots

1 tablespoon freshly-grated ginger
  (or 1 teaspoon dry ginger spice)
4 large egg whites
1 tablespoon oil
1 cup water
2 cups all-purpose flour

Preheat oven to 400° F. Spray 2 6-cup muffin tins with non-stick cooking spray.

Blend the baking powder with the buttermilk. Add the corn syrup, brown sugar, raisins, carrots, ginger, egg whites, oil and water. Stir this mixture well. Gently fold in the flour a little at a time. Mix until the flour is just moistened.

Divide among the muffin tins. Bake 20 minutes, until muffins are lightly browned and firm to the touch. Allow the muffins to cool for 5 minutes before removing from tins.

Muffins may be stored in the refrigerator for up to 3 weeks or in the freezer for 3 months. To reheat, microwave each muffin on high for 30 seconds or heat in a 350° F oven for 10 minutes.

SERVES: 12 ═══════ **NUTRITIONAL INFORMATION PER SERVING** ═══════

Calories	177	Total Fat	2 g	Cholesterol	1 mg
Calories from Fat	8%	Saturated Fat	< 1 g	Sodium	84 mg

APPLESAUCE MUFFINS

Applesauce adds texture and flavor to low-fat foods. Here's a great example.

non-stick cooking spray
1/2 cup 1% buttermilk
1 teaspoon baking powder
1 cup unsweetened applesauce
1/4 cup brown sugar, packed
1 tablespoon cinnamon

1 tablespoon oil
1 teaspoon salt
4 large egg whites
1/2 cup apple juice
2 cups all-purpose flour

Preheat oven to 400° F. Spray 2 6-cup muffin tins with non-stick cooking spray.

Blend the buttermilk with the baking powder. Allow this mixture to sit for 5 minutes or until bubbly.

In a large mixing bowl, blend applesauce, brown sugar, cinnamon, oil, salt, egg whites and apple juice. Mix thoroughly. Fold in the buttermilk mixture. Pour in the flour, a little at a time. Stir until flour is just blended into liquids. Divide into the muffin tins.

Bake at 400° F for 20 minutes until the muffins are lightly browned and firm to the touch. Allow the muffins to cool 5 minutes before removing from tins.

Muffins may be stored in the refrigerator for up to 3 weeks or in the freezer for 3 months. To reheat, microwave each muffin on high for 30 seconds or heat in a 350° F oven for 10 minutes.

SERVES: 12 ═══════ **NUTRITIONAL INFORMATION PER SERVING** ═══════

Calories	120	Total Fat	1 g	Cholesterol	< 1 mg
Calories from Fat	11%	Saturated Fat	< 1 g	Sodium	236 mg

RASPBERRY BANANA MUFFINS

This recipe was published in The New York Times, The Chicago Sun, as well as many other newspapers. These are Mary Ward's signature muffins and they are delicious.

non-stick cooking spray
1 cup 1% buttermilk
1 teaspoon baking powder
1 teaspoon salt
1 tablespoon oil
1/2 cup dark brown sugar,
   firmly packed

1 very ripe banana, mashed
1 pint fresh raspberries
   (or 10 ounces frozen
   raspberries, thawed)
4 large egg whites,
   whipped until soft peaks form
2 cups all-purpose flour

Preheat oven to 400° F. Spray 2 6-cup muffin tins with non-stick cooking spray.

Blend buttermilk with baking powder. Allow this mixture to sit for 5 minutes. Mix in the salt, oil, brown sugar, banana and raspberries. Stir until the mixture is well blended. Fold the raspberry mixture into the egg whites. Gently fold in the flour and mix until just blended with the other ingredients.

Divide this mixture among the muffin tins. Bake 20 minutes or until the muffins are lightly browned and firm to the touch. Allow the muffins to cool for 5 minutes before removing from tins.

Muffins may be stored in the refrigerator for up to 3 weeks or in the freezer for 3 months. To reheat, microwave each muffin on high for 30 seconds or heat the muffins in a 350° F oven for 10 minutes.

SERVES: 12 ═══════ **NUTRITIONAL INFORMATION PER SERVING** ═══════

Calories	144	Total Fat	2 g	Cholesterol	< 1 mg
Calories from Fat	10%	Saturated Fat	< 1 g	Sodium	239 mg

Salads

The most versatile of dishes. Salads can be assembled from leftovers or created from scratch. A salad can complement the most elegant meal or become a meal on its own. Take some liberty with these recipes, and discover the herbs, spices and other ingredients that make a salad perfect for you.

TACO SALAD

A delicious and popular main dish salad that loses the fat without sacrificing the taste.

4 large flour tortillas
non-stick cooking spray
12 ounces ground turkey breast
2 tablespoons taco seasoning
1 12-ounce can hot chili beans
4 cups lettuce, shredded

2 tomatoes, chopped
2 cups salsa
　(see salsa recipe on page 38)
1/4 cup low-fat Monterey Jack cheese
1/4 cup low-fat Yogurt Cheese,
　(see recipe on page 24)

To make taco shell, use 2 glass bowls that fit inside each other. Spray both sides of tortilla with non-stick cooking spray. Turn one bowl upside down and place the tortilla on it. Put into microwave. Put other bowl, upside down on top; this will give a bowl-shape to the tortilla. Microwave on high for 2 minutes. Carefully remove top bowl – it will be hot. Continue to microwave the taco bowl for an additional 3 to 4 minutes until the taco shell is crispy and browned. Remove and store in a sealed plastic bag.

Allow glass bowls to cool then repeat with other tortillas.

Brown turkey breast meat in a non-stick frying pan. Add taco seasoning and hot chili beans, mashing to make a thick mixture.

To assemble taco salads, divide meat mixture among 4 shells. Top with lettuce, tomatoes, salsa, Monterey Jack cheese and yogurt cheese.

SERVES: 4 ══════════ **NUTRITIONAL INFORMATION PER SERVING** ══════════

Calories	344	Total Fat	7 g	Cholesterol	58 mg
Calories from Fat	18%	Saturated Fat	2 g	Sodium	419 mg

CONFETTI SALAD

This salad makes a colorful presentation. Make it in advance, it will keep for up to 4 days.

3 scallions, sliced
1 teaspoon marjoram
2 teaspoons granulated sugar
1 tablespoon olive oil
1/4 cup red wine or balsamic vinegar
1 medium zucchini,
    scrubbed and grated with skin

1 10-ounce package frozen
    cut corn, thawed
1 medium-sized red pepper, seeded
    and chopped into 1/2-inch pieces
salt and pepper to taste

In a medium-sized bowl, blend the scallions, marjoram, granulated sugar, olive oil and vinegar. Add zucchini, corn and red pepper. Chill for at least 1 hour. Salt and pepper to taste.

SERVES: 4	NUTRITIONAL INFORMATION PER SERVING				
Calories	110	Total Fat	2 g	Cholesterol	0 mg
Calories from Fat	18%	Saturated Fat	< 1 g	Sodium	8 mg

CORN AND BLACK BEAN SALAD

The blend of vegetables and herbs combined with a touch of olive oil results in a flavorful salad.

1 10-ounce package frozen white
    or yellow corn, cooked
1 16-ounce can black beans, drained
1 4-ounce can mild or
    hot green chilies, minced

1 tablespoon olive oil
1/4 cup cilantro, chopped
4 scallions, minced
lettuce leaves, sliced radishes and
    cilantro sprigs for garnish

Blend all ingredients and chill for 1 hour.

To Serve: Place on small lettuce leaves garnished with sliced radishes and a sprig of cilantro.

SERVES: 6	NUTRITIONAL INFORMATION PER SERVING				
Calories	87	Total Fat	1 g	Cholesterol	0 mg
Calories from Fat	10%	Saturated Fat	< 1 g	Sodium	618 mg

FIFTEEN-BEAN SALAD

If you don't have packaged fifteen-bean mix in your market, try blending your own favorite beans. Fifteen-bean mix includes: great northern beans, pintos, small reds, large limas, baby limas, black-eyed peas, light red kidneys, garbanzos, Michigan navies, black beans, small pinks, small whites, white kidneys, plus lentils, green split peas and whole green peas.

With so many different sizes of beans, it is important to give the beans an overnight soak. Our fifteen-bean mixture (after an overnight presoak) cooked in 45 minutes. The beans should be evenly cooked and tender, not mushy.

12 ounces fifteen-bean mix
1 medium red onion, thinly sliced
1 red pepper, seeded
   and chopped into 1/2-inch pieces
2 tablespoons vegetable oil
1/2 cup freshly squeezed
   lemon juice with pulp

1/2 teaspoon Worcestershire sauce
1/4 cup granulated sugar
1 clove garlic, minced
1/3 cup parsley, chopped
salt and pepper to taste
lettuce leaves for garnish
lemon slices for garnish

Rinse and sort beans. Place the beans in a medium-sized saucepan and cover with 4 cups water. Allow to soak overnight.

Drain and rinse beans. Cover with fresh water. Bring to a boil, cover and simmer for 45 minutes to 1 hour, until the beans are just cooked. Make sure beans are covered with 1/2 cup water at all times. Drain and cool. Add the onion and red pepper and toss to mix.

In a small mixing bowl, whisk together the vegetable oil, lemon juice, Worcestershire sauce, sugar and garlic. Toss with cooled bean mix and chopped parsley. Salt and pepper to taste.

Chill for at least 4 hours, preferably overnight, before serving.

To Serve: Line a large bowl with lettuce leaves. Arrange salad in the bowl. Garnish with thinly-sliced lemon.

SERVES: 6 ══ **NUTRITIONAL INFORMATION PER SERVING** ══

Calories	283	Total Fat	6 g	Cholesterol	0 mg
Calories from Fat	19%	Saturated Fat	< 1 g	Sodium	22 mg

EGGPLANT SALAD

Art Ulene's favorite snack food.

1 large eggplant
1 teaspoon olive oil
1 clove garlic, minced

salt to taste
crushed red pepper to taste

Preheat oven to 450° F. Put whole eggplant on a pan, prick with fork and bake with skin on until soft, 30 to 45 minutes. Remove from oven and cool. Cut off stem and peel away all skin.

With a food processor or by hand, mash the eggplant until extremely fine. Add olive oil and garlic and mix well. Salt to taste. Sprinkle with crushed red pepper to taste. Chill in refrigerator.

As a salad, serve on lettuce or endive leaves. To use as an appetizer, serve as a dip with vegetable crudité or melba rounds.

SERVES: 4 ══ **NUTRITIONAL INFORMATION PER SERVING** ══

Calories	53	Total Fat	1 g	Cholesterol	0 mg
Calories from Fat	17%	Saturated Fat	< 1 g	Sodium	3 mg

MINTED CITRUS SALAD

Satisfying but light, this salad combines two excellent sources of Vitamin C. Make sure you include orange pulp in the dressing.

Dressing
1/3 cup granulated sugar
1/2 cup water
3 tablespoons fresh mint sprigs
  or 1 tablespoon dry mint leaves)
juice of 1 orange, including pulp

1 grapefruit, peeled and cut into 6 slices
2 small oranges,
  peeled and cut into 4 slices
mint sprigs for garnish

In a small saucepan, combine sugar and water. Stir to dissolve sugar. Bring to a boil. Remove from heat and add mint. Allow to cool for 1 hour.

Strain dressing and add orange juice. Meanwhile, arrange grapefruit and orange slices on 2 plates. Top with 3 to 4 tablespoons dressing and garnish with mint.

Refrigerate any remaining dressing for up to 1 week.

SERVES: 2 ══════ **NUTRITIONAL INFORMATION PER SERVING** ══════

Calories	247	Total Fat	< 1 g	Cholesterol	0 mg
Calories from Fat	1%	Saturated Fat	< 1 g	Sodium	2 mg

HOT CHICKEN SALAD

Delectable and filling, a "salad" that might be called a casserole by some. Whatever category you place it in, it's a winner!

non-stick cooking spray
2 cups cooked chicken breast meat,
   cubed (about 1 pound raw)
1 teaspoon salt
2 cups celery, chopped
1 small green pepper,
   seeded and chopped

1 small onion, chopped
1 1/2 cups chicken stock
   (homemade or prepared)
1/4 cup all-purpose flour
1/4 cup cheddar cheese, grated
2 tablespoons almonds, slivered
1 cup nonfat potato chips, crushed

Preheat oven to 350° F. Coat a 9 x 9-inch baking dish with non-stick cooking spray. Blend chicken breasts with salt, celery, green pepper and onion. Set aside.

In a small saucepan, heat stock. Whisk in flour and cook into a smooth, thickened sauce. Pour over chicken and into prepared dish. Top with grated cheese, almonds and potato chips. Bake for 30 minutes. Serve hot or cold.

SERVES: 6 ═══ **NUTRITIONAL INFORMATION PER SERVING** ═══

Calories	186	Total Fat	4 g	Cholesterol	32 mg
Calories from Fat	19%	Saturated Fat	< 1 g	Sodium	496 mg

RICE AND FRUIT SALAD

Here's a salad for people with a sweet tooth. It's beautiful to look at and very crunchy to the taste.

1 cup raw rice, cooked until just tender
1 teaspoon olive oil
3 cups fresh or canned fruit such as
   halved strawberries, mandarin orange
   segments, fresh pineapple, fresh
   peaches, fresh pears, bananas
1/4 cup granulated sugar

1/2 teaspoon dry mustard
1/2 teaspoon salt
1 tablespoon onion, grated
juice of 4 limes
2 teaspoons fruity olive oil
1/2 teaspoon poppy seeds
2 tablespoons pecan halves

Cook rice just until tender, then add 1 teaspoon olive oil to it. Cool. Blend fruit lightly. In a small bowl, whisk together sugar, dry mustard, salt, onion, lime juice, fruity olive oil and poppy seeds. Blend fruit, rice and dressing. Refrigerate.

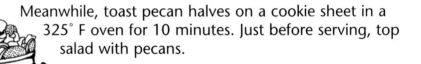

Meanwhile, toast pecan halves on a cookie sheet in a 325° F oven for 10 minutes. Just before serving, top salad with pecans.

SERVES: 6 ═══════════ **NUTRITIONAL INFORMATION PER SERVING** ═══════════

Calories	220	Total Fat	5 g	Cholesterol	0 mg
Calories from Fat	20%	Saturated Fat	< 1 g	Sodium	191 mg

PAPAYA SALAD

A refreshing and exotic salad that is a perfect summertime dish.

3 papayas, peeled, seeded and sliced
juice of 1 lemon
1 cup nonfat yogurt
1/4 teaspoon thyme

freshly ground black pepper to taste
1/4 teaspoon curry powder
2 bunches watercress

Sprinkle papaya slices with lemon juice. Process the yogurt, thyme, pepper and curry powder briefly in food processor or blender. Place papaya slices on a bed of watercress and drizzle with yogurt dressing.

SERVES: 6		NUTRITIONAL INFORMATION PER SERVING			
Calories	55	Total Fat	< 1 g	Cholesterol	0 mg
Calories from Fat	12%	Saturated Fat	0 g	Sodium	31 mg

TOMATO SALAD

You can't beat the flavor of a home-grown tomato and this recipe makes the most of that home-grown taste!

2 tomatoes
freshly grated pepper
1/2 teaspoon fruity olive oil
1 clove garlic, minced
3 tablespoons balsamic vinegar
1 teaspoon fresh basil, chopped

1 teaspoon Worcestershire sauce
thyme sprigs
3/4 teaspoon salt
4 scallions, chopped
1 tablespoon sugar

Slice tomatoes and place in a medium-sized bowl. Combine remaining ingredients and pour over tomatoes. Refrigerate for 1 hour. Serve on a bed of greens.

SERVES: 4		NUTRITIONAL INFORMATION PER SERVING			
Calories	35	Total Fat	1 g	Cholesterol	0 mg
Calories from Fat	20%	Saturated Fat	< 1 g	Sodium	417 mg

POTATO SALAD

Potato salad is an all-time favorite. In place of bacon fat, sour cream and mayonnaise, this recipe uses low-fat French onion dip, yogurt cheese and mustard.

6 medium-sized, all-purpose potatoes,
   about 2 pounds, well-scrubbed
3 quarts water
1/4 cup white wine vinegar
1 small onion, grated
1 teaspoon prepared mustard
   (preferably Dijon)
1/2 cup low-fat French onion chip dip
1/2 cup Yogurt Cheese
   (see recipe on page 24)

1/2 cup chopped fresh herbs
   (parsley, basil, oregano and/or chives)
6 scallions, sliced
1 carrot, grated
2 hard-boiled eggs, chopped
3 ribs celery, diced
1 tablespoon dill pickle relish
sliced radishes for garnish
parsley sprigs or fresh dill for garnish

Scrub the potatoes. In a 1-gallon stockpot filled with 3 quarts boiling water, cook the potatoes with their skins. Cook just until tender. Cool until able to handle, then cut into 1-inch cubes.

Combine vinegar, onion, mustard, chip dip, yogurt cheese, herbs and scallions and pour over the cooked potatoes to marinate. When this mixture has cooled, add the carrot, eggs, celery and relish. Refrigerate until cold, about 3 hours.

Garnish with radish slices and parsley sprigs or fresh dill.

SERVES: 6 ═══════════ **NUTRITIONAL INFORMATION PER SERVING** ═══════════

Calories	187	Total Fat	3 g	Cholesterol	73 mg
Calories from Fat	16%	Saturated Fat	< 1 g	Sodium	574 mg

TABBOULI

The primary ingredient in tabbouli is bulgur wheat. It is used as "rice" in the Middle East and has a distinct nutty flavor.

1 cup bulgur wheat, soaked in boiling
  water for 1 hour
2 large tomatoes, skinned, seeded and
  finely chopped
1 cup parsley, finely chopped
2 tablespoons mint, finely chopped
1 bunch scallions, sliced
juice of 3 limes

1 tablespoon fruity olive oil
1 teaspoon salt
1/2 teaspoon cumin
1/4 teaspoon turmeric
mint sprigs and cherry tomato halves
  for garnish
6 pita rounds

Drain the bulgur well. Add tomatoes, parsley, mint and scallions. Make dressing by combining lime juice, olive oil, salt, cumin and turmeric. The tabbouli salad may be made up to a day in advance to this point.

To Serve: Blend bulgur mixture with dressing. Decorate serving bowl or platter with additional sprigs of mint and cherry tomato halves. Serve with pita wedges.

SERVES: 6 ══════════ **NUTRITIONAL INFORMATION PER SERVING** ══════════

Calories	195	Total Fat	3 g	Cholesterol	0 mg
Calories from Fat	14%	Saturated Fat	< 1 g	Sodium	795 mg

TUNA SALAD

This salad is great in pita sandwiches, tuna melts, stuffed into tomatoes or right out of the bowl on crackers. You can eliminate the chopped egg if you want to cut fat just a little more.

2 3-ounce cans water-packed
  tuna, undrained
1/4 cup low-fat French onion dip
2 tablespoons dill pickle relish
2 scallions, sliced
1 rib celery, diced

1 tablespoon chopped sweet
  or Jalapeño pepper
1 hard-boiled egg, chopped
2 pita rounds
lettuce and tomato

Blend tuna with dip, relish, scallions, celery, pepper and chopped egg. Stuff into pita rounds and add lettuce and tomato.

SERVES: 2 ══════ **NUTRITIONAL INFORMATION PER SERVING** ══════

Calories	283	Total Fat	6 g	Cholesterol	144 mg
Calories from Fat	19%	Saturated Fat	2 g	Sodium	803 mg

CHICKEN SESAME SALAD

With its array of Asian flavors and satisfying ingredients, this popular salad is a lunch or dinner favorite.

2 chicken breasts (12 ounces),
  skinned, boned and marinated for
  up to 3 days in the juice of a lime,
  2 crushed garlic cloves, 1/4 cup
  chicken stock and 2 tablespoons
  tamari or low-sodium soy sauce
2 cups tiny peas, fresh or frozen
1 pound bow-tie pasta

1 bunch scallions, sliced
4 ounces canned pimiento, with liquid
4 ounces sliced water
  chestnuts, drained
1 tablespoon sesame seeds, toasted
additional tamari
  or soy sauce, if desired

Poach the chicken in the marinade until just cooked, about 10 minutes. Cool and slice into chunks, reserving hot liquid.

Cook peas until just tender and cook pasta according to package directions.

To assemble salad, blend chicken breast chunks with peas, pasta, scallions, pimiento with liquid, water chestnuts and reserved hot marinade. Allow to chill several hours, then top with sesame seeds. Serve extra tamari or soy sauce on the side.

SERVES: 4	NUTRITIONAL INFORMATION PER SERVING				
Calories	334	Total Fat	3 g	Cholesterol	23 mg
Calories from Fat	8%	Saturated Fat	< 1 g	Sodium	197 mg

WALDORF TURKEY SALAD

Traditional Waldorf Salad is laden with heavy salad dressing and walnuts. This version reduces the fat while preserving the crisp apple flavor!

1/4 cup low-fat mayonnaise
1/2 cup nonfat yogurt
1 1/2 cups cooked turkey breast,
   cubed or shredded
1 tablespoon granulated sugar
4 large, red or yellow Delicious apples
   (about 2 pounds), cored and cubed

juice of 1 lemon
1 cup celery, chopped
1/2 cup raisins
4 medium-sized lettuce cups
1/4 cup chopped walnuts, toasted

Combine the mayonnaise, yogurt, turkey and granulated sugar.

Toss the apples with the lemon juice to prevent browning. Add the celery and raisins. Fold the turkey-yogurt mixture over apple mixture. Chill for at least 1 hour. Toast walnuts in the oven at 325° F for 10 minutes.

To Serve: Divide salad among 4 lettuce cups. Top with toasted walnuts.

SERVES: 4	NUTRITIONAL INFORMATION PER SERVING				
Calories	315	Total Fat	6 g	Cholesterol	76 mg
Calories from Fat	18%	Saturated Fat	1 g	Sodium	188 mg

Meats

Both red and white meats can be included in a healthy low-fat diet. Always buy the leanest meat possible and trim away all visible fat. Choose "select" cuts when possible as they are lower in fat than "choice" or "prime" meats. If taste is important, use the prime meat but cut the portion size.

BEEF BURGUNDY WITH ROSEMARY

A traditional favorite, slow-cooked in a tasty burgundy sauce.

2 pounds lean beef roast
  (round or bottom round)
slivers of garlic and rosemary
1 rib celery, chopped
3 carrots, chopped

1 cup good quality Burgundy wine
1 cup beef stock
4 cups cooked rice
sprigs of rosemary for garnish

Preheat oven to 250° F. Tie the beef into an oblong with a diameter of about 5 inches. Make a series of slices about 1/2-inch deep into the meat. Fill those slices with slivers of garlic and rosemary. Place the meat in a covered baking dish with vegetables, wine and stock; cover and bake, very slowly, for 3 hours.

Drain Burgundy sauce from the meat and purée it in a blender.

To Serve: Place a serving of rice on each plate, top with slices of beef and the Burgundy purée. Garnish with additional rosemary.

SERVES: 6 ===== **NUTRITIONAL INFORMATION PER SERVING** =====

Calories	368	Total Fat	8 g	Cholesterol	100 mg
Calories from Fat	19 %	Saturated Fat	3 g	Sodium	96 mg

VEAL SCALOPPINE

This is a meal for a hearty appetite. The contrast of crispy veal and soft, flavorful potatoes is delicious.

12 veal medallions
  (about 1 1/2 pounds)
1/2 cup flour
1 egg
2 egg whites
1 1/4 cups seasoned, dry bread crumbs
1 1/2 teaspoons dry oregano

1 teaspoon black pepper
2 teaspoons olive oil
12 small red-skin potatoes,
  boiled and sliced
6 lemon wedges
parsley sprigs for garnish

With a meat mallet or the side of a small plate, pound veal to 1/4-inch thick.

Place the flour on a plate. Stir egg and egg whites together in medium-sized bowl. Blend dry bread crumbs with oregano and black pepper and put on a plate. Coat medallions with flour, then egg, then bread crumbs.

Heat a large, non-stick frying pan over medium heat and add the oil. When the oil is hot, add the veal medallions and cook until golden, about 3 minutes per side.

To Serve: Fan potato slices around plate. Top with veal medallions and garnish with lemon wedges and parsley sprigs.

SERVES: 6 ═══════════ **NUTRITIONAL INFORMATION PER SERVING** ═══════════

Calories	431	Total Fat	9 g	Cholesterol	132 mg
Calories from Fat	19%	Saturated Fat	2 g	Sodium	256 mg

BEEF FILLET WITH HOT CAJUN FRIES

Small, tender steaks served in a nest of Cajun Fries, make this a quick and hearty meal.

2 large baking potatoes
2 tablespoons Cajun seasoning
2 tenderloin steaks (4 ounces each)
   from the very center of the tenderloin

a few gourmet mushrooms, sliced
parsley sprigs for garnish

Cut potatoes into 1-inch slices and sprinkle with Cajun seasoning. Place on a metal steak plate or heat-proof platter. Heat broiler.

Broil potatoes until they are nicely browned and tender, about 10 minutes. The plate will be very hot. Broil or grill steaks until they have reached the desired degree of doneness. Grill mushroom slices for the last few minutes.

To Serve: Place steak on platter with potatoes. Top with mushroom slices. Garnish with parsley sprigs.

SERVES: 2 ═══ **NUTRITIONAL INFORMATION PER SERVING** ═══

Calories	460	Total Fat	8 g	Cholesterol	71 mg
Calories from Fat	15%	Saturated Fat	3 g	Sodium	70 mg

BEEF TIPS WITH NOODLES

If you buy whole beef tenderloin, cut away all fat and membrane, then divide into small steaks. The head and the tail of the tenderloin do not make nice steaks, so cut them away and enjoy them in this recipe.

2 cups beef stock
  (homemade or prepared)
8 ounces tenderloin tips
  (or any lean steak) cut into
  2-inch pieces

4 cups cooked noodles
chopped parsley for garnish

Heat beef stock. Heat a medium-sized, non-stick frying pan to hot. Place tenderloin tips in it, turning them until they brown to the desired degree of doneness.

To Serve: Mix stock with noodles. Top with tenderloin tips and chopped parsley.

SERVES: 4 ═══ **NUTRITIONAL INFORMATION PER SERVING** ═══

| Calories | 320 | Total Fat | 7 g | Cholesterol | 97 mg |
| Calories from Fat | 19% | Saturated Fat | 2 g | Sodium | 42 mg |

BRAISED FLANK STEAK
WITH PASTA AND TOMATOES

Few recipes allow you to braise flank steak without oil. This one does, and it is excellent. In fact, it's essential to the recipe that you not use oil, so follow the directions closely.

12-ounce package pasta
　(orzo or a small soup pasta)
2 cloves garlic, minced
1 large onion, thinly sliced
3 tablespoons peppercorns

1 flank steak (1 pound)
2 cups dry white wine, divided
15-ounce can tomato sauce
　(salt-free), divided
5 tablespoons basil, shredded, divided

Cook pasta until al dente (about 8 minutes). Drain and keep warm.

In a non-stick, medium-sized saucepan, poach garlic and onion in tomato sauce, until onion becomes translucent. Simmer.

Crush peppercorns in coffee mill, processor or with a rolling pin. Rub into both sides of flank steak. In a heavy, non-stick skillet, sear meat until it is deep brown on both sides (5 minutes). Add 1/2 cup wine to deglaze pan. Add remaining wine into the tomato sauce and simmer.

When wine has deglazed pan, pour half of tomato sauce into pan. Top with half of shredded basil, continuing to simmer. Add cooked pasta to remaining tomato sauce. Top with basil.

To Serve: Carve meat in thin slices, cutting diagonally across the grain of the meat. Arrange cooked pasta onto serving platter. Top with meat and tomato sauce. Sprinkle with remaining basil.

SERVES: 4	NUTRITIONAL INFORMATION PER SERVING				
Calories	344	Total Fat	7 g	Cholesterol	38 mg
Calories from Fat	17%	Saturated Fat	3 g	Sodium	81 mg

CHATEAUBRIAND

It's become a culinary style to layer entrées with a starchy vegetable and a combination of other vegetables. This technique makes the total recipe low-fat if the proportion of the starchy vegetable and the meat are about the same, so that the low-fat content of the one offsets the high-fat content of the other.

2 large baking potatoes	baby vegetables
1/2 cup low-fat yogurt	(eggplant, squash, carrots)
salt and pepper to taste	parsley sprigs
2 tenderloin steaks (4 ounces each) from the very center of the tenderloin	

Preheat oven to 350° F. Allow the potatoes to bake until very tender, about 45 minutes to 1 hour. When potatoes have cooled to touch, scoop out the hot flesh. Add yogurt to the scooped-out potato, mash and then salt and pepper to taste. Divide potatoes into 2 portions and scoop onto a metal steak pan or oven-proof plate. Make a well in the center of the potatoes for the meat.

Heat broiler, then broil potatoes until they are nicely browned and plate is very hot. Remove potatoes and broil or grill steaks until they have reached the desired degree of doneness. Broil baby vegetables for the last few minutes.

To Serve: Place cooked tenderloin in the potato well. Place parsley sprigs on the side of the plate with the baby vegetables.

SERVES: 2 ══════════ **NUTRITIONAL INFORMATION PER SERVING** ══════════

Calories	495	Total Fat	9 g	Cholesterol	75 mg
Calories from Fat	16%	Saturated Fat	3 g	Sodium	109 mg

BEEF FAJITAS

The marinade and preparation method for Beef Fajitas will work just as well with chicken breast or pork tenderloin.

12 ounces beef flank steak
1 large onion, sliced
1 red pepper, sliced
1 green pepper, sliced
8 flour tortillas
2 cups chili beans (hot or mild)

Toppings
Yogurt Cheese (see recipe on page 24)
salsa (see recipe on page 38)
chopped cilantro
sliced green onions
chopped Jalapeño peppers

Marinade
juice of 2 limes
1/4 cup beef stock
1/2 cup beer
1/4 cup cilantro, chopped

Reserve 1/4 cup of the marinade. Using the rest of the marinade, marinate meat for at least 2 hours or up to 2 days. Broil or grill meat 4 inches from heat until desired degree of doneness is reached, about 5 minutes per side for rare, more for medium or well-done. Meanwhile, using a non-stick pan, poach onion and peppers in 1/4 cup of the marinade.

To Serve: Warm tortillas. Slice meat into thin slices. Place 1/4 cup beans, 1 scoop of pepper mix and a few slices of meat into each tortilla. Top with favorite toppings.

SERVES: 8 ══════ **NUTRITIONAL INFORMATION PER SERVING** ══════

Calories	174	Total Fat	4 g	Cholesterol	21 mg
Calories from Fat	20%	Saturated Fat	1 g	Sodium	28 mg

RAINBOW STUFFED PEPPERS

With so many beautiful and colorful sweet peppers available, you'll be able to create a masterpiece of color with this recipe and it tastes as good as it looks!

non-stick cooking spray
1 cup bulgur wheat, soaked in boiling
　water for 1 hour
6 large sweet peppers
　(green, red, yellow)
12 ounces very lean ground sirloin

1/2 cup onion, chopped
2 cloves garlic, minced
2 large tomatoes, chopped
1 teaspoon ground oregano
1 teaspoon hot sauce
2 teaspoons white Worcestershire sauce

Preheat the oven to 350° F. Spray a 9 x 13-inch baking dish with non-stick cooking spray.

Cut the tops from the peppers. Discard the seeds and membranes from the interior of the peppers. Chop enough of the tops to make 1/2 cup. Set

aside. Cook the peppers in boiling water for 3 minutes until they are tender. Drain well.

In a large-sized skillet, brown the ground beef, onion, garlic and chopped pepper until meat is brown and vegetables are tender. Drain fat from pan. Add the tomatoes, oregano, hot sauce and Worcestershire. Simmer for 15 minutes until flavors are well blended. Remove from heat and add drained bulgur wheat.

Stuff peppers with meat mixture. Place in a baking dish and cover with aluminum foil. Bake, covered, for 30 minutes. Serve immediately.

SERVES: 6 ══════ **NUTRITIONAL INFORMATION PER SERVING** ══════

Calories	154	Total Fat	4 g	Cholesterol	33 mg
Calories from Fat	18%	Saturated Fat	1 g	Sodium	57 mg

LAMB CURRY

The use of cracked mustard seed, fresh ginger and fresh curry powder gives this traditional recipe a real "kick".

1 teaspoon olive oil
1/2 teaspoon mustard seed
1 large onion, diced
3 cloves garlic, minced
1 1/2 tablespoons fresh ginger, grated
1 bay leaf
1/4 cup chicken stock
   (homemade or prepared)

2 to 4 tablespoons good quality
   curry powder
12 ounces lean, raw lamb cubes
   (preferably from the leg of lamb)
1/2 cup low-fat yogurt
3 medium-sized tomatoes, diced
1/2 to 1 cup water
4 cups cooked rice
chopped cilantro for garnish

In a large, non-stick frying pan, heat oil to medium hot. Add mustard seed and heat until cracked. Add onion and cook until browned. Lower heat, add garlic and ginger and sauté for an additional minute. Add bay leaf, chicken stock and curry powder and stir to blend.

Increase heat and add lamb cubes, stirring well to mix with the seasonings. Add yogurt, tomatoes and 1/2 to 1 cup water to make a thick sauce. Cover and cook, stirring occasionally, until the meat is tender and the gravy thick.

To Serve: Divide rice among 4 plates. Sprinkle with cilantro. Top with curry.

SERVES: 4 ═══════ **NUTRITIONAL INFORMATION PER SERVING** ═══════

Calories	401	Total Fat	9 g	Cholesterol	58 mg
Calories from Fat	19%	Saturated Fat	3 g	Sodium	83 mg

THE BEST BARBECUE SAUCE

This barbecue sauce has lots of ingredients and is really delicious. It keeps well and can be used for beef, pork, chicken or veal.

1 teaspoon olive oil
1 medium onion, chopped
2 cloves garlic, minced
2 tablespoons white vinegar
1 cup black coffee
1 teaspoon Dutch cocoa
1/2 cup beer
1 cup chili sauce
1/4 cup light soy sauce
juice and grated peel of 1/2 lemon
2 tablespoons Worcestershire sauce

2 tablespoons steak sauce
few drops hot pepper sauce
1 tablespoon dry mustard
1/4 teaspoon of all or any of the
   following: celery seed, thyme,
   turmeric, marjoram, paprika,
   red pepper, ginger
2 tablespoons horseradish
2 bay leaves
2 teaspoons cornstarch

In a medium-sized, non-stick saucepan, heat oil. Sauté onion and garlic for 2 minutes. Reduce heat and blend in remaining ingredients, whisking in the cornstarch last. Simmer for 1 hour.

Recipe makes 3 cups (24 1-ounce servings).

SERVES: 24 ═══════ **NUTRITIONAL INFORMATION PER SERVING** ═══════

Calories	28	Total Fat	< 1 g	Cholesterol	0 mg
Calories from Fat	9%	Saturated Fat	< 1 g	Sodium	425 mg

THE BEST BARBECUED PORK

Serve barbecued pork with hominy, which will absorb that wonderful barbecue sauce.

1 pound pork tenderloin,
  cleaned of all fat and membrane
2 cups The Best Barbecue Sauce
  (see recipe on page 114)

1 16-ounce can white hominy
thin slices of lime for garnish
herb sprigs for garnish

Marinate pork tenderloin in barbecue sauce for at least 2 hours or up to 2 days. Grill or broil pork tenderloin 4 inches from heat until well-done, turning often (this will take about 25 minutes). Heat remaining barbecue sauce.

To Serve: Cut pork into thin slices and put onto warmed plates with a serving of hominy. Pour barbecue sauce over the pork with a little on the hominy. Garnish with thin slices of lime and herb sprigs.

SERVES: 4 ===== **NUTRITIONAL INFORMATION PER SERVING** =====

Calories	249	Total Fat	5 g	Cholesterol	6 mg
Calories from Fat	18%	Saturated Fat	1 g	Sodium	425 mg

PORK STIR-FRY

Almost any vegetable can be used in this recipe. Fresh green beans or pea pods work especially well.

3 tablespoons cornstarch, divided
2 tablespoons tamari
  or light soy sauce, divided
1 clove garlic, minced
1/2 teaspoon dry mustard
12 ounces pork tenderloin,
  cleaned and sliced into thin strips
  (or pork stir-fry meat)
2 teaspoons oil
1 cup chicken stock
  (homemade or prepared)

4 cups sliced fresh vegetables,
  such as green beans cut on the
  diagonal, fresh peas, chopped celery,
  bamboo shoots, sliced scallions, sliced
  zucchini, sliced sweet pepper
1 cup water chestnuts,
  sliced and drained
1/2 cup white wine
sliced hot peppers or Jalapeños to taste
4 cups steamed white rice

Combine 1 tablespoon of cornstarch with tamari or soy sauce, garlic and mustard. Coat sliced pork with the mixture.

Heat a large, non-stick frying pan or skillet and add oil. Add pork and stir-fry until meat is cooked. Remove pork and add stock. Add vegetables and cook until tender.

Blend remaining tamari or soy sauce and remaining cornstarch with white wine. Whisk into vegetable mixture, cooking until it thickens. Add pork to heat, then serve over rice.

SERVES: 4		NUTRITIONAL INFORMATION PER SERVING			
Calories	441	Total Fat	8 g	Cholesterol	59 mg
Calories from Fat	14%	Saturated Fat	2 g	Sodium	571 mg

SHISH KEBOB

Lamb makes an authentic shish kebob and the leg of the lamb is lower in fat than many other meats. You can substitute lean pork, chicken or beef.

1 pound lamb (preferably from the leg), cut into 1-inch cubes
1/2 cup white wine
1/2 cup chicken stock (homemade or prepared)
6 cloves garlic, minced
4 scallions, sliced
2 tablespoons fresh mint, chopped, divided

1 cup nonfat yogurt
6-inch bamboo skewers
2 teaspoons fresh or dry oregano
12 cherry tomatoes
12 button mushrooms
12 small onions, blanched
1 green pepper, cut into 16 pieces
1 zucchini, cut into 16 pieces
12 small new potatoes, blanched

Toss the meat with wine, stock, garlic, scallions and 1 tablespoon mint. Cover and refrigerate for 2 hours or overnight. Blend yogurt with remaining mint.

Preheat grill or broiler. Skewer meat and vegetables onto separate skewers – all meat, all tomato, all potato, etc. Broil or grill 4 inches from heat about 5 minutes per side for lamb and potatoes, less for the vegetables. When meat and vegetables have finished cooking, remove from skewers and place on a large serving platter or bowl. Serve with yogurt.

SERVES: 6	NUTRITIONAL INFORMATION PER SERVING				
Calories	278	Total Fat	6 g	Cholesterol	54 mg
Calories from Fat	19%	Saturated Fat	2 g	Sodium	81 mg

Poultry

Poultry continues to grow in popularity. Leaner than red meat, poultry is versatile, relatively inexpensive and delicious. Chicken and turkey breast are the leanest cuts and are used often in the following recipes.

Always keep these tips in mind: Remove poultry skin before eating, not before cooking. The skin will seal in moisture throughout the cooking process and the fat will not penetrate the meat. Buy only ground turkey labeled "lean ground turkey breast meat" to avoid having the fatty skin ground in with the meat. Turkey ground with skin can have nearly as much fat as ground beef.

BAKED TARRAGON CHICKEN

Delightful to eat, this recipe is sure to be a favorite.

2 whole chicken breasts,
  skinned and boned
1/4 teaspoon dried tarragon
freshly ground black pepper to taste
non-stick cooking spray
1/4 cup chicken broth
1 teaspoon tomato paste

1 tablespoon tarragon vinegar
1 garlic clove, mashed
lettuce, endive and/or
  other fresh greens
green onion tops, chopped
2 cups cooked rice

Preheat oven to 375° F. Sprinkle each breast with tarragon and pepper. Spray a non-stick frying pan with non-stick cooking spray. Sear both sides of each breast, pressing down on the meat with a spatula until browned. Remove from heat.

Transfer chicken to a shallow roasting pan. In the same frying pan, mix together chicken broth, tomato paste, tarragon vinegar and garlic, using wooden spoon to stir and scrape bits of chicken from the pan bottom. Pour over chicken breasts and bake 25 to 30 minutes, or until juices run clear when breast is pricked with a fork.

To Serve: Arrange lettuce, endive and/or other greens on serving platter. Top with chicken breasts and sauce. Garnish with green onion tops. Serve with rice on the side.

SERVES: 4 ═══ **NUTRITIONAL INFORMATION PER SERVING** ═══

Calories	245	Total Fat	3 g	Cholesterol	54 mg
Calories from Fat	4%	Saturated Fat	1 g	Sodium	114 mg

CHICKEN POT PIE

Almost any vegetable can be substituted for the peas and carrots in this recipe.

2 whole chicken breasts,
  with skin and bone (about 2 pounds)
3 cups chicken stock
  (homemade or prepared)
2 onions, diced
2 carrots, chopped
3 ribs celery, sliced
1/2 cup cold water

1/3 cup cornstarch
1 10-ounce package frozen peas
2 cups all-purpose flour
2 teaspoons baking powder
1 teaspoon salt
1 egg, beaten
1 tablespoon oil
1 cup cold nonfat milk

In a large soup pot, combine chicken breasts with chicken stock, onions, carrots and celery. Heat to a boil, then gently poach chicken until tender, about 30 minutes. Remove chicken; cool, skin and debone. Slice into 1-inch chunks.

Reduce chicken stock to 2 cups, then thicken chicken stock by whisking in cornstarch that has been blended with 1/2 cup cold water. Add chicken chunks and peas.

Preheat oven to 400° F. Blend flour with baking powder and salt. Mix egg with oil and milk. Blend the wet ingredients into the dry ingredients until flour is just moistened. Mixture will be sticky. Pour chicken into a 2-quart casserole.

Drop biscuit mixture atop chicken by spoonfuls. Bake until puffed and brown, about 20 to 25 minutes.

SERVES: 6 ═══════ **NUTRITIONAL INFORMATION PER SERVING** ═══════

Calories	296	Total Fat	3 g	Cholesterol	35 mg
Calories from Fat	9%	Saturated Fat	< 1 g	Sodium	588 mg

HONEY-LIME-ROSEMARY ROAST CHICKEN
WITH OVEN-BROWNED POTATOES

When you need a change from chicken breasts, try this favorite recipe. It is unbelievably tender and moist. Make sure some of the marinade drips and coats the oven-browned potatoes.

1 whole chicken (4 pounds)	4 tablespoons honey
1 lime, thinly sliced	juice of 4 limes
4 sprigs rosemary, separated into leaves	rosemary, lime pieces and Italian
3 large baking potatoes, halved	parsley for garnish

Preheat oven to 400° F. Remove all visible fat from chicken. Force lime slices and rosemary leaves up under the skin of the chicken and place the remainder into the cavity.

Arrange chicken and potato halves, cut side up, in a roasting pan. Bake for 20 minutes or until chicken starts to brown. Mix honey and lime juice.

Reduce heat to 350° F and baste the chicken and potatoes with the honey and lime juice mixture. Baste frequently until chicken is deeply glazed and the juices of the thigh run clear when punctured with a fork. Remove all skin and carve chicken.

To Serve: Place chicken pieces and potatoes on a serving platter garnished with additional lime slices, rosemary and Italian parsley.

Variation: When in season, red bliss potatoes and homegrown baby vegetables are a superb complement to this dish.

SERVES: 4		NUTRITIONAL INFORMATION PER SERVING			
Calories	533	Total Fat	11 g	Cholesterol	138 mg
Calories from Fat	19%	Saturated Fat	3 g	Sodium	127 mg

CRISPY "FRIED" CHICKEN

This "frying" technique simulates the crunch of fried foods and can be used in other entrées such as veal chops, pork chops or catfish. Vary the spice, but always use 1% buttermilk to marinate.

1/2 cup 1% buttermilk
1 tablespoon Worcestershire sauce
1/4 teaspoon (or less) cayenne pepper

2 whole chicken breasts
 (1 1/2 pounds), boned and skinned
3 cups low-fat crispy-flaked cereal
 non-stick cooking spray

Blend buttermilk with Worcestershire sauce and cayenne pepper. Marinate chicken in this sauce for at least 4 hours or up to 2 days. Preheat oven to 400° F. Spray a baking sheet with non-stick cooking spray.

Crush cereal and place it in a shallow bowl. Coat each chicken piece thoroughly with cereal flakes. Bake 25 to 30 minutes until chicken is just tender and serve.

SERVES: 4		NUTRITIONAL INFORMATION PER SERVING			
Calories	154	Total Fat	2 g	Cholesterol	52 mg
Calories from Fat	14%	Saturated Fat	< 1 g	Sodium	203 mg

Marinated Chicken

Marinating chicken results in a moister and more tender chicken breast. This is especially important when the chicken is poached and used, for example, in a salad.

The following marinades really penetrate and flavor the chicken. These marinades also work very well with pork tenderloin and beef flank steak.

ORANGE WHISKEY MARINADE

1 cup orange juice
2 tablespoons honey
4 cloves garlic, crushed
crushed pepper flakes

fresh ginger root
2 tablespoons whiskey
4 chicken breasts (about 1 1/2 pounds),
 boned and skinned

Combine ingredients for marinade. Marinate chicken for at least 4 hours or up to 4 days.

Grill, broil or sauté chicken with a little oil in a non-stick frying pan.

SERVES: 4		NUTRITIONAL INFORMATION PER SERVING			
Calories	165	Total Fat	2 g	Cholesterol	51 mg
Calories from Fat	13%	Saturated Fat	< 1 g	Sodium	46 mg

TERIYAKI MARINADE

2 tablespoons light soy sauce
1/2 cup chicken stock
 (homemade or prepared)
2 tablespoons dry sherry
1 tablespoon prepared mustard

1 tablespoon brown sugar
juice of 2 lemons or limes
4 chicken breasts (about 1 1/2 pounds),
 boned and skinned

Combine ingredients for marinade. Marinate chicken for at least 4 hours or up to 4 days.

Grill, broil or sauté chicken with a little oil in a non-stick frying pan.

SERVES: 4		NUTRITIONAL INFORMATION PER SERVING			
Calories	134	Total Fat	2 g	Cholesterol	51 mg
Calories from Fat	15%	Saturated Fat	< 1 g	Sodium	303 mg

CHICKEN WITH TOMATOES, PEPPERS AND MUSHROOMS

This recipe has intense flavor generated by caramelizing the chicken pieces after they have been coated with tomato paste.

2 teaspoons olive oil, divided
2 cloves garlic, minced
1/2 cup mushrooms,
  cut into 1/4-inch pieces
6 ounces tomato paste, canned
2 chicken leg-thigh quarters and
  1 whole chicken breast, skinned
2 green peppers, cut into 1/2-inch strips

1 red pepper, cut into 1/2-inch strips
1 cup mushrooms, sliced
4 large tomatoes, seeded and chopped
freshly grated black pepper
6 ounces dry white wine
2 tablespoons parsley, chopped
2 tablespoons basil, chopped
2 cups rice, cooked

In a frying pan, heat 1 teaspoon oil until hot. Add garlic and mushrooms and sauté until mushrooms are cooked and all oil has been absorbed. Remove to a plate.

Heat remaining oil until hot. Place tomato paste onto a plate. Coat chicken pieces with tomato paste and add to the frying pan. Brown on both sides, caramelizing the tomato paste. This takes about 15 minutes. Add peppers, mushrooms, tomatoes, freshly ground pepper and white wine into the frying pan, cover and allow to simmer for 35 minutes.

Remove chicken pieces and debone. Place chicken back into the sauce with reserved mushroom-garlic mixture. When ready to serve, sprinkle with parsley and basil and serve with rice.

SERVES: 4 ═══════ **NUTRITIONAL INFORMATION PER SERVING** ═══════

| Calories | 283 | Total Fat | 5 g | Cholesterol | 34 mg |
| Calories from Fat | 17% | Saturated Fat | 1 g | Sodium | 82 mg |

CHICKEN PICCATA WITH SAFFRON RICE

A lemon-laced dish with a hint of fire.

4 chicken breasts, boned and skinned
  (about 1 1/2 pounds)
1/4 cup all-purpose flour
1/8 teaspoon red pepper flakes
1 teaspoon oil

1 cup chicken stock
  (homemade or prepared)
juice of 1 lemon
lemon slices
2 cups rice, cooked with
  a pinch of saffron

With a meat cleaver or the side of a small plate, pound the chicken breasts until very thin. Blend flour with pepper flakes. Coat chicken breasts with this mixture.

In a non-stick frying pan, heat oil to hot. Cook chicken breasts about five minutes per side. Chicken is done when the interior meat is white with no trace of pink. Remove chicken and keep it warm. Heat stock in frying pan and add lemon juice. Cook until all the browned bits are dissolved and stock is reduced by half.

To Serve: Mound rice on a serving plate. Top with chicken, lemon slices and sauce.

SERVES: 4 ═══════════ **NUTRITIONAL INFORMATION PER SERVING** ═══════════

Calories	285	Total Fat	5 g	Cholesterol	69 mg
Calories from Fat	16%	Saturated Fat	< 1 g	Sodium	68 mg

CHICKEN ENCHILADAS

Cooking chicken in a delicious pepper-onion mixture gives it a rich flavor with no added fat!

2 teaspoons olive oil, divided
1 onion, chopped
2 cloves garlic, chopped
1 1/2 pounds tomatillos, peeled,
   washed and quartered
   (or 16-ounce jar salsa verde)
1 Jalapeño pepper, chopped and seeded
1 1/2 cups water, divided
1 large red onion, sliced
1 large red pepper, seeded and sliced

2 cups chicken stock, divided
1 whole chicken breast (about 1 pound)
   with skin and bone
1 teaspoon ground cumin
1 teaspoon chili powder
1/4 cup cilantro, shredded
1/4 cup Italian parsley, chopped
3 tablespoons cornstarch
1/2 cup water
8 flour tortillas

In a heavy, non-stick saucepan, heat 1 teaspoon oil. Brown onion and garlic. Add tomatillos, Jalapeño and 1 cup water. Cover and simmer for 15 minutes. In a medium frying pan, heat remaining teaspoon of olive oil. Add onion and red pepper and allow to brown slowly until they caramelize, about 30 minutes. Carefully remove the tomatillo mixture to a blender or a food mill. Blend or mill, then strain to remove seeds and heavy skin. Return mixture to saucepan. Divide chicken stock between the saucepan and the frying pan.

Meanwhile, add chicken, cumin, chili powder, cilantro and parsley to the mixture in the frying pan. Simmer until chicken is cooked, about 20 minutes. Remove chicken, remove skin, debone, shred and add back to mixture. Blend cornstarch with 1/2 cup water. Whisk 2/3 of it into the tomatillo mixture. Whisk remainder into the chicken mixture. As the mixture heats and thickens, heat flour tortillas.

To Serve: Divide chicken mixture among 8 flour tortillas. Roll, place on plate and top with tomatillo sauce.

SERVES 8 ═══════════ **NUTRITIONAL INFORMATION PER SERVING** ═══════════

Calories	376	Total Fat	7 g	Cholesterol	46 mg
Calories from Fat	17%	Saturated Fat	< 1 g	Sodium	55 mg

FIESTA CHICKEN

This simple recipe is very attractive and tasty.

2 whole chicken breasts (about 1 1/2
    pounds), boned and skinned
juice of 1 lemon
3 cloves garlic, crushed
1 1/2 cups chicken stock
    (homemade or prepared)
3/4 cup raw rice
2 ribs celery, finely chopped

1 medium-sized green pepper,
    seeded and finely chopped
1 medium-sized tomato, seeded
    and finely chopped
2 scallions, sliced
hot pepper sauce
1 teaspoon oil

Coat chicken breasts with lemon and garlic. Marinate for at least 4 hours or up to 2 days.

Heat stock and cook rice until tender, about 45 minutes. While hot, add celery, peppers, tomatoes, scallions and hot pepper sauce. In a non-stick frying pan, heat oil. Sauté chicken breasts until browned and cooked through, about 30 minutes.

To Serve: Cover a medium-sized platter with the rice. Top with chicken pieces.

SERVES: 4	NUTRITIONAL INFORMATION PER SERVING		
Calories	216	Total Fat	3 g	Cholesterol	4 mg
Calories from Fat	12%	Saturated Fat	< 1 g	Sodium	28 mg

QUICK AND EASY TURKEY LOAF

This turkey loaf is tastier than meat loaf. It is light and flavorful with a good texture.

1 cup nonfat milk
1/4 cup tomato paste
2 egg whites
4 slices stale bread, torn
non-stick cooking spray

1 pound lean-ground turkey
  breast meat
1 onion, chopped
1 green or red pepper, seeded
  and chopped

Blend milk with tomato paste, egg whites and bread. Allow to set for 30 minutes.

Preheat oven to 350° F. Spray a 9 x 5 x 3-inch loaf pan with non-stick cooking spray. Mix ground turkey breast with onion and pepper. Add tomato mixture and mix well. Pack into loaf pan. Bake 45 minutes.

SERVES: 4	NUTRITIONAL INFORMATION PER SERVING	
Calories 246	Total Fat 2 g	Cholesterol 72 mg
Calories from Fat 7%	Saturated Fat < 1 g	Sodium 244 mg

TURKEY CROQUETTES

This is a recipe that children love to help make and eat.

2 medium baking potatoes
1 pound lean ground turkey
  breast meat
1 tablespoon Italian parsley, chopped
1 onion, grated
1/2 teaspoon nutmeg
1 egg
2 egg whites

1/4 cup flour
1 tablespoon oil
1/2 cup well-seasoned chicken stock
  (homemade or prepared)
2 tablespoons cornstarch
1 teaspoon butter
chopped Italian parsley for garnish

Preheat oven to 350° F. Bake potatoes until tender, about 45 minutes to an hour. In a non-stick frying pan, brown ground turkey breast. Add parsley and onion and cook until onion is translucent.

Scoop potato flesh out of potatoes and into a large bowl. Sprinkle with nutmeg and mash with a fork. Add cooled turkey meat mixture, egg and egg whites and blend thoroughly. Form 12 oval-shaped croquettes, each about 2 inches long. Coat with flour. Heat oil in non-stick frying pan and brown croquettes on both sides, about 5 minutes per side.

Meanwhile, blend stock with cornstarch in a non-stick saucepan. Heat and whisk until thickened. Add butter.

To Serve: Make a pool of thickened chicken stock on each plate. Sprinkle with Italian parsley and top with 3 hot turkey croquettes.

SERVES: 4 ══════ **NUTRITIONAL INFORMATION PER SERVING** ══════

Calories	302	Total Fat	6 g	Cholesterol	127 mg
Calories from Fat	18%	Saturated Fat	2 g	Sodium	91 mg

ROAST TURKEY BREAST
WITH CORNMEAL STUFFING

Here's a sumptuous holiday meal that is not devastating to a sensible eating plan.

1 turkey breast with bone and a full
   covering of skin, about 4 pounds
fresh sage or other herb leaves
1 6-ounce package sage stuffing mix
1 2-ounce cornmeal muffin, crumbled
1 small zucchini, shredded
1 medium onion, chopped fine
2 stalks celery, chopped fine

1 egg, slightly beaten
4 to 5 cups chicken stock
   (homemade or prepared)
1 cup water
1/3 cup white flour
orange slices, cranberries,
   herb leaves to garnish platter

Preheat oven to 350° F. Place turkey breast on a roasting pan. Loosen skin from turkey breast and place herb leaves under skin. Roast turkey breast to medium stage, about 1 hour 30 minutes to 1 hour 45 minutes.

Blend stuffing mix, muffin, zucchini, onion, celery, egg and 2 cups chicken stock. Place in a baking dish, cover with foil, place in oven along with the turkey breast and bake for 1 hour 15 minutes.

When turkey breast tests barely done on a meat thermometer (about 165° F), remove from oven and place turkey under a foil tent to keep warm. To make gravy, add 1 cup water to drippings in pan and heat, scraping all the flavorful bits from the pan. Blend flour with remaining chicken stock and slowly whisk this into the roux in the pan. Whisk until smooth and thick, about 5 minutes.

To Serve: Remove skin and slice turkey into 12 thin slices. Place stuffing on one end of warmed platter with turkey slices on other end. Garnish platter with orange slices, cranberries and herbs. Serve turkey gravy on the side.

SERVES: 6   **NUTRITIONAL INFORMATION PER SERVING**

Calories	413	Total Fat	4 g	Cholesterol	180 mg
Calories from Fat	9%	Saturated Fat	< 1 g	Sodium	637 mg

TURKEY TETRAZZINI

This all-time recipe is a great way to use leftover turkey breast.

1/2 cup dry white wine
3/4 pound sliced mushrooms
2 cups chicken stock
   (homemade or prepared)
3 tablespoons cornstarch
3 cups turkey breast, cubed

1/2 pound noodles, cooked according
   to package directions
1/2 cup half-and-half
non-stick cooking spray
2 tablespoons parmesan cheese, grated

Preheat oven to 375° F. In a large, non-stick frying pan, heat wine. Add mushrooms and poach until tender, about 5 minutes. Blend cornstarch with chicken stock and add it to the mushroom pan. Begin heating, whisking to make a thick sauce. Add turkey and noodles, stirring to distribute all ingredients evenly. Add half-and-half.

Pour mixture into a 2 1/2-quart casserole dish that has been sprayed with non-stick cooking spray. Sprinkle with parmesan cheese and bake for 20 to 25 minutes until heated through and browned.

SERVES: 6 ═══ **NUTRITIONAL INFORMATION PER SERVING** ═══

Calories	341	Total Fat	5 g	Cholesterol	15 mg
Calories from Fat	13%	Saturated Fat	2 g	Sodium	131 mg

Fish & Shellfish

There are as many reasons to eat seafood as there are delicious kinds of seafood to eat. Fish and shellfish are rich with protein and many essential nutrients such as iron, zinc and vitamins D and B.

Unlike many other protein sources, fish and shellfish are low in cholesterol-raising saturated fat. Yet this doesn't mean that seafood is fat-free. In fact, the range of fat content in seafood is tremendous. For example, pike contains only 7% of its calories from fat while salmon contains over 30% fat calories.

Seafood with less than 20% of its calories from fat includes monkfish, water-packed tuna, rockfish, snapper, sole, octopus, flounder, farm-fed catfish, clams, crayfish, shrimp, lobster, perch, pollock, grouper, scallops, cod, haddock, surimi (fake crabmeat) and fresh tuna. Feel free to substitute different kinds of fish when making many of the recipes in this chapter.

CAJUN CRABMEAT STUFFED SNAPPER

Fresh snapper is readily available at most market seafood counters. Haddock or halibut are also good choices for this recipe.

non-stick cooking spray
2 teaspoons olive oil, divided
1/4 cup onion, minced
1/4 cup celery, chopped
2 tablespoons fresh parsley, chopped
1 garlic clove, minced
2 tablespoons Cajun seasoning, divided
1 tablespoon all-purpose flour

1/2 cup dry white wine
1/2 cup cooked crabmeat, fresh,
  frozen or canned
4 red snapper fillets,
  about 7 ounces each
lemon wedges for garnish
parsley sprigs for garnish

Preheat oven to 400° F. Spray a cookie sheet with non-stick cooking spray.

Heat 1 teaspoon oil and sauté onion, celery, parsley and garlic until the onion is translucent. In a small bowl, mix 1 tablespoon Cajun seasoning and flour with white wine. Whisk into the onion mixture, cooking until smooth and thick. Add the crabmeat.

Spread 1/3 cup crabmeat mixture onto each snapper fillet. Wrap into a bundle. Brush with remaining teaspoon olive oil and coat well with remaining tablespoon Cajun seasoning. Place on cookie sheet and bake 10 to 12 minutes. The snapper is ready when the flesh just flakes.

Serve on a heavy platter garnished with lemon and parsley.

SERVES: 4 ═══ **NUTRITIONAL INFORMATION PER SERVING** ═══

Calories	231	Total Fat	3 g	Cholesterol	91 mg
Calories from Fat	20%	Saturated Fat	< 1 g	Sodium	255 mg

CIOPPINO WITH BRUSCHETTA

This makes a large kettle of a most fragrant stew. Add a pinch of saffron and call it Bouillabaisse – or add cayenne pepper and call it Spicy Cioppino.

1 teaspoon plus 1 tablespoon olive oil
4 cloves garlic, minced
1 pound scrubbed clams
1 cup dry white wine
1 1/2 pounds scrubbed mussels
3 large tomatoes
1/4 cup basil leaves
1 cup chicken stock
   (homemade or prepared)

1 1/2 pounds cod fillets,
   cut into 1-inch pieces
1 pound medium shrimp,
   peeled but raw

Bruschetta
8 thick slices Italian bread
4 cloves garlic, sliced

In a heavy stockpot, heat teaspoon of olive oil. Add garlic and sauté until garlic is brown.

Add clams and wine. Cover, bring to a boil and cook for 5 minutes or until all clams are open. Remove clams, add mussels and repeat until mussels are open. Remove mussels.

Meanwhile, purée tomatoes with basil and tablespoon of olive oil. Add tomato purée with chicken stock to the seafood broth. Bring to a boil, add cod fillets and simmer for 2 minutes. Add shrimp and simmer for 3 minutes until they are just cooked. Add clams and mussels and heat through.

Make bruschetta by rubbing Italian bread with garlic slices and toasting the bread. For each serving, place a piece of bruschetta into a large, shallow bowl and top with cioppino.

SERVES: 8 ═══════════ **NUTRITIONAL INFORMATION PER SERVING** ═══════════

Calories	223	Total Fat	3 g	Cholesterol	102 mg
Calories from Fat	14%	Saturated Fat	< 1 g	Sodium	314 mg

SHRIMP WITH ARTICHOKE HEARTS

Artichoke hearts always seem to add a gourmet accent. In this recipe, their unique texture and flavor, combined with white wine, mushrooms and shrimp, turn a great dish into a fabulous one (see color photo on page 166).

1 teaspoon olive oil
2 cups fresh mushrooms, sliced
2 cloves garlic, chopped
bunch of scallions, sliced
3/4 cup dry white wine

2 tablespoons basil, chopped
6 ounces artichoke hearts,
  packed in water, drained
1 pound shrimp, with shells

Heat oil in a heavy, non-stick frying pan. Add mushrooms and sauté until brown. Add garlic, scallions, wine, basil and artichoke hearts and simmer until hot. Add shrimp and cook 4 to 5 minutes until they turn bright pink. Serve shrimp unpeeled or peeled with steamed pea pods and rice.

SERVES: 4	NUTRITIONAL INFORMATION PER SERVING		
Calories	110	Total Fat	2 g	Cholesterol	117 mg
Calories from Fat	18%	Saturated Fat	< 1 g	Sodium	142 mg

CRUNCHY CATFISH FILLETS

The mild flavor of fresh, farm-grown catfish is pleasing to most people. A few spices and some cornmeal will add flavor without fat. This is also a good recipe to try on the charcoal grill.

10 ounces fresh, farm-grown catfish
  fillets, rinsed
1 cup 1% buttermilk
1/2 cup yellow cornmeal

1/2 teaspoon freshly ground
  black pepper
1/2 teaspoon Hungarian paprika
1/4 teaspoon cayenne pepper
non-stick cooking spray

Soak catfish in buttermilk for at least 30 minutes. Combine cornmeal with peppers and paprika. Heat oven to broil. Spray a broiling pan with non-stick cooking spray. Drain most of the buttermilk from catfish. Roll in cornmeal mixture. Broil 3 to 4 minutes per side. When fish flakes easily, it is ready to serve.

SERVES: 2		NUTRITIONAL INFORMATION PER SERVING			
Calories	301	Total Fat	4 g	Cholesterol	99 mg
Calories from Fat	11%	Saturated Fat	1 g	Sodium	224 mg

HALIBUT WITH CONFETTI SAUCE

Baking seafood with fresh vegetables makes so much sense – the vegetables moisten and flavor the mild fish without adding fat (see color photo on page 167).

4 halibut steaks, about 6 ounces each
juice of 1 lemon
salt and pepper to taste
4 scallions, chopped
4 carrots, peeled and shredded

1/4 cup Italian parsley, chopped
3 tablespoons fresh dill, chopped
2 large tomatoes, peeled and chopped
1/2 cup fresh bean sprouts
1 lemon, wedged

Preheat oven to 350° F.

Place halibut in baking dish and season with lemon juice, salt and pepper. In a bowl, toss together scallions, carrots, parsley and dill. Spoon over fish.

Cover and bake for 20 minutes or until fish flakes with a fork.

To Serve: Garnish with tomato, bean sprouts and lemon wedges.

SERVES: 4		NUTRITIONAL INFORMATION PER SERVING			
Calories	235	Total Fat	4 g	Cholesterol	54 mg
Calories from Fat	16%	Saturated Fat	< 1 g	Sodium	123 mg

POACHED SALMON FILLETS
WITH SWEET PEPPER AND ZUCCHINI

This recipe is so beautiful, you'll feel like an artist when you make it.

4 salmon fillets (1 1/2 pounds)
1 onion, cut into thirds
3 tablespoons dry tarragon
3 cups chicken stock
   (homemade or prepared)
2 tablespoons dry dill
4 sprigs of dill for garnish
4 red-skin potatoes,
   cooked with skins, sliced

Red and Green Sauces
2 roasted red peppers
2 tablespoons chicken stock
   (homemade or prepared), divided
1 medium-sized zucchini
salt and pepper to taste

To make red sauce, purée roasted red peppers with 1 tablespoon chicken stock. Salt and pepper to taste.

To make green sauce, steam zucchini for 5 minutes, until soft. Purée with remaining tablespoon of chicken stock. Salt and pepper to taste.

Place salmon in a heavy frying pan with onion, tarragon, 3 cups chicken stock and dry dill. Cover, heat and poach gently for about 10 minutes until fish just flakes.

To Serve: Put red sauce on one side of plate, green sauce on the other. Put salmon on top of the sauces. Garnish with dill and frame with potato slices.

SERVES: 4 ═══════ **NUTRITIONAL INFORMATION PER SERVING** ═══════

Calories	384	Total Fat	11 g	Cholesterol	126 mg
Calories from Fat	16%	Saturated Fat	2 g	Sodium	100 mg

SCALLOP AND LEMON SHRIMP SKEWERS

Scallops and shrimp cook very quickly, so they're a perfect pair in a recipe for the grill.

1 pound scallops
  (use bay scallops, if possible)
juice of 2 limes
2 cloves garlic, minced
4 sprigs fresh rosemary
2 teaspoons honey
1/4 cup dry white wine

1 pound jumbo shrimp
  (about 16) in the shell
juice of 1 lemon
1 teaspoon olive oil
2 tablespoons cilantro, chopped
1/2 cup chicken stock
  (homemade or prepared)
8 bamboo skewers, about 8 inches long

Marinate scallops in lime juice, garlic, rosemary, honey and wine. Marinate at least 2 hours or up to 12 hours.

Marinate shrimp in lemon juice, olive oil, cilantro and chicken stock. Marinate at least 2 hours or up to 12 hours.

Thread onto 8 skewers, alternating shrimp and scallops. Grill over a hot fire or broil in the oven, brushing scallops and shrimp with marinade frequently.

To Serve: Serve over a bed of lemon couscous or risotto.

SERVES: 4 ═══════════ **NUTRITIONAL INFORMATION PER SERVING** ═══════════

Calories	206	Total Fat	3 g	Cholesterol	168 mg
Calories from Fat	12%	Saturated Fat	< 1 g	Sodium	334 mg

SHRIMP AND FETA

For this recipe, it's really important to start with a great feta cheese, available in supermarkets or in gourmet cheese stores.

2 pounds unpeeled, raw shrimp (medium-sized)

1/4 cup onion, finely chopped

4 large tomatoes, skinned, seeded and chopped

1/2 cup dry white wine

1 tablespoon fresh oregano, chopped (dry is fine)

3 tablespoons parsley, chopped

4 ounces feta cheese, crumbled

salt and pepper to taste

6 crusty slices French bread

Shell and devein shrimp, leaving tails on. In a large, non-stick frying pan, mix onion, tomatoes, wine, oregano and parsley. Cook until the tomatoes form a light purée. Add shrimp and cook just until shrimp turns pink, about 5 minutes. Add feta cheese and salt and pepper to taste.

To Serve: Divide among 6 ramekins and serve with plenty of French bread to sop up the delicious juice.

SERVES: 6 ═══ **NUTRITIONAL INFORMATION PER SERVING** ═══

Calories	244	Total Fat	5 g	Cholesterol	185 mg
Calories from Fat	20%	Saturated Fat	3 g	Sodium	556 mg

STIR-FRY HUNAN SHRIMP

Serve over rice or crunchy noodles. The Oriental flavors are delectably bold.

12 ounces large, raw shrimp, peeled
  and deveined
1 teaspoon fresh ginger, minced
1 clove garlic, minced
1 tablespoon tomato paste
2 teaspoons sugar

juice of 1 lemon
1 teaspoon oil
1 medium onion, chopped
2 scallions, chopped
1 tablespoon cornstarch
  dissolved in 1 tablespoon water

Mix raw shrimp with ginger, garlic, tomato paste, sugar and lemon juice.

Heat oil in a wok or in a large non-stick frying pan.
Add shrimp mixture and cook until shrimp turns
pink, about 5 minutes. Remove shrimp.

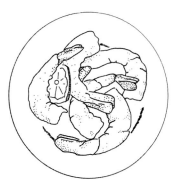

Add onion and scallion and stir fry for 5 minutes.
Add cornstarch, stirring to make a smooth sauce.
Add shrimp, stirring to coat.

Serve immediately.

SERVES: 2	NUTRITIONAL INFORMATION PER SERVING				
Calories	227	Total Fat	4 g	Cholesterol	277 mg
Calories from Fat	16%	Saturated Fat	< 1 g	Sodium	326 mg

TUNA BRUSCHETTA

A different twist on the tuna melt.

1 3 1/2-ounce can
  water-packed tuna, drained
1/2 cup low-fat mozzarella
  cheese, shredded
4 fresh plum tomatoes, chopped
1 small onion, minced
2 teaspoons parsley, chopped

1 teaspoon oregano, chopped
4 1-inch thick slices Italian bread
1/2 teaspoon olive oil
4 cloves garlic, sliced
cherry tomatoes for garnish
oregano sprigs for garnish

Combine cheese with tuna, tomatoes, onion, parsley and oregano.

Brush bread on both sides with olive oil. Rub bread well with sliced garlic.

Heat a non-stick frying pan. Grill bread until light golden brown. Turn and top each toasted bread slice with 1/4 of the tuna-cheese mixture. Continue to grill until cheese melts and bread is golden brown on the bottom.

To Serve: Garnish with cherry tomatoes and oregano sprigs.

SERVES: 4 ═══ **NUTRITIONAL INFORMATION PER SERVING** ═══

Calories	263	Total Fat	6 g	Cholesterol	26 mg
Calories from Fat	20%	Saturated Fat	3 g	Sodium	464 mg

STUFFED RAINBOW TROUT

A change from the usual fare, a nice stuffing adds a distinctive air to the trout.

6 whole small trout, cleaned
   and boned, 5 to 6 ounces each
non-stick cooking spray
1 cup onions, finely chopped
2 ribs celery, chopped
1/2 cup green peppers, chopped

1 medium zucchini, scrubbed
   and grated with peel
2 cloves garlic, minced
1/2 pound tiny cooked shrimp
2 cups fresh bread crumbs
2 egg whites

Preheat oven to 350° F. Wash whole trout and pat dry.

Spray a large, non-stick frying pan with non-stick cooking spray. Add the onions, celery, peppers, zucchini and garlic and cook for 3 minutes. Add the shrimp and bread crumbs and blend well. Beat the egg whites and add to the shrimp mixture. Chill.

Spray a baking pan with non-stick cooking spray. Stuff each trout cavity with 1/6 of the stuffing. Place the trout on the baking pan and bake 25 minutes. The stuffing should be hot and the fish should just flake when pricked with a fork. Serve immediately.

SERVES: 6 ===== **NUTRITIONAL INFORMATION PER SERVING** =====

Calories	230	Total Fat	5 g	Cholesterol	80 mg
Calories from Fat	20%	Saturated Fat	1 g	Sodium	141 mg

SOLE WITH GREEN BEANS AND BASIL

Use any mild white fish for this recipe. Cook just until fish flakes, about 10 minutes.

4 sole fillets (about 1 1/2 pounds)
juice of 3 lemons
1 cup dry white wine, divided
2 teaspoons olive oil, divided
1 small onion, chopped
1 carrot, chopped

1 rib celery, chopped
1/2 cup water
2 cups fresh green beans,
   cleaned and cut to 1-inch lengths
1/4 cup chopped basil

Marinate sole fillets in the juice of one lemon and 1/3 cup wine.

In a large, non-stick frying pan, heat 1 teaspoon olive oil. Sauté onion, carrot and celery until soft. Add 1/3 cup wine and 1/2 cup water and bring to a boil. Reduce sauce by half, strain and reserve liquid.

Add remaining olive oil to frying pan. Drain marinade from sole and save liquid. Sauté sole for 3 minutes. Add remaining wine, cover and simmer for 7 more minutes. Remove fillets and keep warm.

Pour marinade and reserved fish stock into frying pan. Remove from heat. Purée basil leaves and the combined cooking stock.

Steam green beans until tender.

To Serve: Place green beans around the side of a heated plate. Pour a little sauce on the plate and top with a sole fillet.

SERVES: 4 ═══════ **NUTRITIONAL INFORMATION PER SERVING** ═══════

Calories	243	Total Fat	5 g	Cholesterol	86 mg
Calories from Fat	18%	Saturated Fat	< 1 g	Sodium	154 mg

SWORDFISH STEAK WITH TOMATOES, CAPERS AND BLACK OLIVES

The blend of tomatoes, capers and Greek black olives pleases the eye and the continental flavor distinguishes this swordfish dish.

1 medium onion, chopped
2 tomatoes, chopped
2 tablespoons black Greek Calamata olives, pitted and sliced
dash cayenne pepper
1 tablespoon capers
2 tablespoons chopped mint

non-stick cooking spray
2 swordfish steaks, about 12 ounces
2 tablespoons flour
juice of 1 lemon
2 cups cooked risotto
mint sprigs for garnish

Blend onion, tomatoes, black olives, cayenne pepper, capers and mint in a large, non-stick frying pan. Cover and simmer, then remove tomato mixture from frying pan. Clean frying pan. Spray with non-stick cooking spray.

Coat swordfish steaks with flour. Place swordfish steaks in frying pan and sauté until one side is browned. Turn, reduce heat, sprinkle with lemon, add tomato mixture, cover and simmer for about 5 more minutes.

To Serve: Divide risotto between 2 plates. Top with swordfish steaks and vegetables. Garnish with mint sprigs.

SERVES: 2	NUTRITIONAL INFORMATION PER SERVING				
Calories	550	Total Fat	11 g	Cholesterol	66 mg
Calories from Fat	18%	Saturated Fat	2 g	Sodium	424 mg

WHITE FISH WITH PESTO

Pesto presents a great alternative dressing for seafood. This recipe is great with any of the lean fishes, including snapper, sole, rockfish, flounder and haddock.

2 white fish fillets, about 12 ounces
juice of 1 lemon
basil sprigs for garnish

Pesto Sauce:
1 1/2 teaspoons fruity olive oil
1 teaspoon chicken stock
2 cloves garlic, peeled and sliced
1 1/2 teaspoons pine nuts, toasted
1/4 cup basil leaves
1 1/2 teaspoons Italian parsley

Preheat oven to 450° F. Blend pesto ingredients until smooth. Place fillets in an oven-proof baking dish. Squeeze lemon juice over fish. Spread pesto over fish. Bake until fish just flakes, about 10 minutes.

To Serve: Place on heated plates with sprigs of basil for garnish.

SERVES: 2 ══════════ **NUTRITIONAL INFORMATION PER SERVING** ══════

Calories	197	Total Fat	4 g	Cholesterol	152 mg
Calories from Fat	17%	Saturated Fat	< 1 g	Sodium	118 mg

WHITE FISH BAKED IN PARCHMENT PAPER

It's fun to watch this recipe cook – the parchment paper puffs and swells in the oven. Use any white fish such as sole, flounder, perch, pollock or snapper for this recipe. The sauce in this meal is incredible!

2 large squares (12 x 12-inch)
   parchment paper (or aluminum foil)
4 small white fish fillets,
   about 12 ounces
2 medium-sized potatoes, sliced thin
2 plum tomatoes, peeled and chopped

4 Greek Calamata olives,
   sliced and pitted
1/4 cup Italian parsley, chopped
salt and pepper to taste
1/4 cup dry white wine
juice of 1 lemon
1 egg white

Preheat oven to 400° F. Place parchment paper on working surface. Top with 2 small fish fillets. Cover with half of potato, tomatoes, olives, parsley, salt and pepper. Sprinkle with half of wine and lemon juice.
Repeat with second parchment square.

Pleat and fold parchment paper to ensure that all edges are sealed. After sealing, rub a little egg white on folds and pleats. During baking, this will act as glue. Place parchment packages on a baking sheet and bake 25 minutes.

To Serve: Place parchment package on each plate. Open and enjoy.

SERVES: 2 ======= **NUTRITIONAL INFORMATION PER SERVING** =======

Calories	345	Total Fat	3 g	Cholesterol	152 mg
Calories from Fat	8%	Saturated Fat	< 1 g	Sodium	201 mg

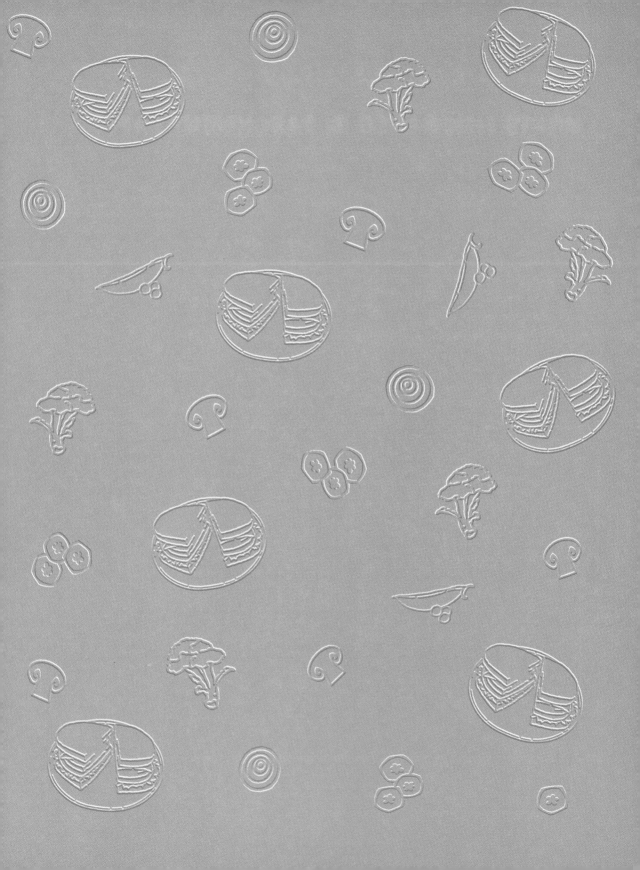

Sandwiches

Sandwiches are a staple of the American diet. With a little imagination and a few minutes, almost any ingredient can become part of a delicious sandwich.

Instead of bread, use pita pockets or tortillas. For fillings, give a lift to standard sandwich fare with Cajun Chicken, Mushroom Stuffing or a homemade Veggie Burger. Enjoy this selection of low-fat combinations and experiment to create your own.

AVOCADO AND SPROUT SANDWICH

Avocado is full of fat, but it has wonderful texture and flavor. Here, just a bit of avocado makes for a healthy snack or sandwich.

2 slices whole-grain bread
1/2 teaspoon low-fat mayonnaise
1 slice avocado (1/2 ounce)
2 slices very ripe tomato
1/4 cup sprouts (spicy or mung)

gourmet lettuce (arugula or red tip)
1/4 cucumber, sliced
red onion, a few very thin slices
beaumonde seasoning (onion-celery
    blend found in spice section)

Toast bread. Spread one side with mayonnaise. Layer other ingredients, sprinkling all with beaumonde. Top with other slice of bread. Eat and enjoy.

SERVES: 1 ════════ **NUTRITIONAL INFORMATION PER SERVING** ════════

Calories	233	Total Fat	35 g	Cholesterol	1 mg
Calories from Fat	19%	Saturated Fat	< 1 g	Sodium	499 mg

BEAN AND CHICKEN BURRITO SUPREME

This recipe is low in fat, full of fiber and hearty enough for a main meal.

1 teaspoon oil
1/2 cup onion, sliced
1/2 cup green pepper, sliced
1 clove garlic, crushed
12 ounces chicken breast, ground
1 tablespoon chili powder
1 teaspoon cumin
1 12-ounce can pinto beans

1 cup brown rice, cooked
1/4 cup chilies, hot or mild
6 whole-wheat tortillas
sliced lettuce and chopped
    tomato for garnish
1 1/2 cups salsa (see recipe on page 38)
1 cup Yogurt Cheese
    (see recipe on page 24)

In a non-stick frying pan, heat oil. Add onion, pepper, garlic and ground chicken and sauté until all pink is gone. Add chili powder, cumin, pinto beans, rice and chilies.

Preheat oven to 350° F. Fill 6 tortillas, each with 1/6 of mixture. Fold sides and roll so that burrito is enclosed. Place on a baking sheet and bake for 10 minutes or until tortilla is crispy.

To Serve: Place a little lettuce and tomato on each plate. Top with hot burritos, salsa and yogurt cheese.

SERVES: 6		NUTRITIONAL INFORMATION PER SERVING			
Calories	288	Total Fat	5 g	Cholesterol	18 mg
Calories from Fat	16%	Saturated Fat	< 1 g	Sodium	113 mg

CAJUN CHICKEN SANDWICH

A spicy Cajun-influenced sandwich. The orange-marinated chicken adds a special tang.

2 teaspoons paprika
a dash to 3/4 teaspoon cayenne pepper
   (depending on desired hotness)
1 teaspoon white pepper
1 teaspoon onion powder
1 teaspoon garlic powder
2 teaspoons dry oregano

2 tablespoons all-purpose flour
4 chicken breasts (1 pound),
   boned, skinned and marinated
   in the juice of 2 oranges for
   at least 2 hours or up to 2 days
4 Kaiser rolls
lettuce and tomato

Preheat oven to 400° F. Combine spices and flour. Drain chicken leaving it a little wet. Coat breasts evenly with the seasoning mixture. Place on a non-stick baking pan and bake for 12 to 15 minutes until the center is no longer pink. (Or you may grill the chicken on a charcoal grill over medium coals for 10 to 15 minutes.)

To Serve: Place on toasted Kaiser rolls and top with lettuce and tomato.

SERVES: 4		NUTRITIONAL INFORMATION PER SERVING			
Calories	377	Total Fat	2 g	Cholesterol	34 mg
Calories from Fat	5%	Saturated Fat	1 g	Sodium	245 mg

PITA STUFFS I

When you're in the mood for a little meat, this is the perfect pita.

1 large whole-wheat pita pocket
1 slice onion
1 slice green pepper
1 slice ripe tomato

1 ounce fat-free ham
1 ounce low-fat mozzarella cheese
shredded basil leaves

Preheat oven to 350° F. Open pita pocket. Stack ingredients in order listed. Close pita, place on an ungreased baking pan and bake for 20 minutes. Serve hot.

SERVES: 1	NUTRITIONAL INFORMATION PER SERVING				
Calories	238	Total Fat	4 g	Cholesterol	17 mg
Calories from Fat	17%	Saturated Fat	< 1 g	Sodium	618 mg

PITA STUFFS II

An all-time favorite sandwich. Try using a wide variety of vegetables but always include onion, garlic and tomato.

non-stick cooking spray
1/2 teaspoon oil
1 medium-sized onion, sliced
1 clove garlic, minced
1 large tomato, chopped
1 large zucchini, scrubbed
   and shredded with skin

1 tablespoon fresh basil, chopped
   (or 1 teaspoon dry basil)
4 pita bread pockets
1 tablespoon parsley, chopped
2 tablespoons parmesan cheese, grated
1/4 cup (2 ounces) part-skim
   mozzarella cheese, shredded
salt and pepper to taste

Preheat oven to 400° F. Spray a baking sheet with non-stick cooking spray.

Heat oil in a medium-sized, non-stick skillet. Add onion and garlic and cook until brown. Add tomato, zucchini and basil. Cover and sauté vegetables for about 6 minutes, until just tender.

Cut the pitas in half. With a slotted spoon, spoon 1/8 of vegetable mixture onto each pita half. Sprinkle with parsley. Blend cheeses and top hot vegetables with cheese mixture. Place on baking sheet and bake until cheese is melted and bubbly, about 8 to 10 minutes. Salt and pepper to taste.

SERVES: 4		NUTRITIONAL INFORMATION PER SERVING			
Calories	238	Total Fat	4 g	Cholesterol	17 mg
Calories from Fat	17%	Saturated Fat	< 1 g	Sodium	618 mg

PITA PIZZA

This pita is quick and easy. Prepared spaghetti sauce is fine when you're short on time, but the recipe is best when you use your own sauce.

non-stick cooking spray
2 pita bread pockets
1/2 cup nonfat spaghetti sauce
1/4 cup corn, frozen, canned or fresh, cooked and drained
1 small zucchini, scrubbed and grated with skin

2 tablespoons part-skim mozzarella cheese, shredded
1 tablespoon parmesan cheese, grated
freshly ground pepper

Preheat broiler. Spray a cookie sheet with non-stick cooking spray. Place the pitas on the cookie sheet and broil 4 inches from source of heat until both sides are crispy, about 5 minutes. Reduce the oven temperature to 350° F. Top each pita with 1/2 of spaghetti sauce, corn and zucchini. Sprinkle with mozzarella and parmesan cheeses.

Bake for 20 minutes. The cheeses should be melted and the vegetables hot. Pepper to taste.

SERVES: 2		NUTRITIONAL INFORMATION PER SERVING			
Calories	181	Total Fat	3 g	Cholesterol	2 mg
Calories from Fat	18%	Saturated Fat	2 g	Sodium	348 mg

SLOPPY JOE

Boldly flavored ingredients make it easy to substitute bulgur wheat for part of the traditional Sloppy Joe ground meat. Bulgur wheat (wheat that has been parboiled) has a soft, grainy consistency that absorbs flavors well.

1 teaspoon oil
1 medium-sized green pepper,
   seeded and finely chopped
1 medium-sized onion,
   cut into small cubes
2 cloves garlic, smashed
1 medium-sized carrot,
   scraped and chopped
1 rib celery, chopped

1 pound lean ground turkey breast
1 8-ounce can tomato sauce
1/2 cup bulgur wheat,
   soaked in boiling water for 1 hour
1/4 cup parsley, chopped
1/2 teaspoon Worcestershire sauce
6 Kaiser rolls
thin slices of onion

Heat oil in a non-stick pan. Add pepper, onion, garlic, carrot and celery and cook until vegetables are tender. Push to side and add turkey breast, crumbling it and cooking it until no pink remains.

Add tomato sauce, bulgur wheat, chopped parsley and Worcestershire sauce. Cover and simmer for an additional 20 minutes for flavors to blend.

To Serve: Toast rolls, spoon on Sloppy Joe and top with thin slices of onion.

SERVES: 6 ══════ **NUTRITIONAL INFORMATION PER SERVING** ══════

Calories	380	Total Fat	4 g	Cholesterol	47 mg
Calories from Fat	9%	Saturated Fat	< 1 g	Sodium	606 mg

ITALIAN BREAD WITH MUSHROOM STUFFING

Mushroom lovers will swear they've gone to heaven after the first bite of this warm, creamy, mushroom sandwich.

1 pound mushrooms (chanterelle, cremini, moonlight or a mixture)
1 teaspoon olive oil
3 scallions, finely sliced
1 tablespoon fresh thyme
4 ounces Canadian bacon, finely chopped

1 cup chicken stock (homemade or prepared)
2 tablespoons cornstarch
1/3 cup Yogurt Cheese (see recipe on page 24)
4 slices Italian bread (2 inches thick)
1 tablespoon fresh thyme for garnish
freshly chopped parsley for garnish

Separate mushroom tops from stems. Chop stems and slice tops. Heat oil in a large non-stick saucepan. Add scallions and thyme and sauté until scallions are transparent. Add Canadian bacon and the mushroom stems and sauté until browned. Next, add mushroom tops and a little water, cover and simmer for 5 minutes or until all vegetables are tender.

Meanwhile, in a small saucepan, make a sauce by whisking the cornstarch into the chicken stock. Heat, whisking constantly until sauce thickens. Add yogurt cheese and warm slightly, then add cream sauce to the mushroom sauce and heat thoroughly.

To Serve: Make a bread bowl out of the Italian bread slices by removing some of the center. Toast. Place on warmed plates and divide mushrooms among the plates. Sprinkle with thyme and parsley.

SERVES: 4 ══════ **NUTRITIONAL INFORMATION PER SERVING** ══════

Calories	283	Total Fat	4 g	Cholesterol	18 mg
Calories from Fat	13%	Saturated Fat	1 g	Sodium	745 mg

TURKEY BURGER

Our nation's favorite food with far less fat. You'll love the flavor of turkey burgers cooked on the grill.

1 pound lean ground turkey breast
1/4 cup green pepper, chopped
1/4 cup red pepper, chopped
1 egg
2 tablespoons seasoned bread crumbs

1/2 teaspoon Worcestershire sauce
4 hamburger buns, toasted
lettuce, tomato and onion
    for topping burgers

Blend turkey breast with peppers, egg, seasoned bread crumbs and Worcestershire sauce. Mix very lightly. Grill over charcoal fire about 4 inches away from heat. Or grill under the broiler about 4 inches away from heat. Do not press down with spatula and turn only one time, about 5 minutes into cooking.

Serve on toasted buns with lettuce, tomato and onion.

SERVES: 4 === **NUTRITIONAL INFORMATION PER SERVING** ===

Calories	346	Total Fat	4 g	Cholesterol	124 mg
Calories from Fat	10%	Saturated Fat	1 g	Sodium	470 mg

QUESADILLA

Here's a favorite quick sandwich, made with ingredients that are easy to keep on hand.

non-stick cooking spray
4 flour tortillas
1/2 cup fresh Tomato Salsa
   (see recipe on page 38)
1/2 cup corn, cooked
1/2 cup chili beans
2 tablespoons low-fat Monterey Jack
   cheese, shredded

Spray a griddle or large skillet with non-stick cooking spray. Heat to hot. Divide salsa between two of the tortillas. Sprinkle each with corn, beans and cheese. Top with remaining tortillas.

Grill, turning once, until tortillas are golden brown and filling is hot. Cut into 8 wedges.

SERVES: 4 === **NUTRITIONAL INFORMATION PER SERVING** ===

Calories	136	Total Fat	3 g	Cholesterol	5 mg
Calories from Fat	19%	Saturated Fat	< 1 g	Sodium	184 mg

VEGGIE BURGER WITH CUCUMBER COULIS

A very tasty burger that can be made any size, from giant (6 per recipe) to mini (48 per recipe).

1 teaspoon oil
1 rib celery, diced
1 large carrot, cubed
1 cup onion, diced
1 cup fresh or frozen peas
1/4 teaspoon red pepper flakes
4 ounces tomato sauce
1/2 cup bulgur wheat soaked in boiling
    water for 1 hour, then drained
3 large egg whites

1 cup seasoned bread crumbs
non-stick cooking spray
6 hamburger rolls

Cucumber Coulis:
1 large cucumber, chopped
1 stalk celery, chopped
3 tablespoons cilantro
1 tablespoon rice vinegar
1/4 cup onion, chopped

Heat oil in a large non-stick skillet and sauté vegetables until tender, 10 to 15 minutes. Transfer to a large bowl and add red pepper flakes, tomato sauce, bulgur wheat, egg whites and bread crumbs. Form into 6 large veggie burgers.

Clean out pan, spray with non-stick cooking spray and sauté burgers about 5 minutes per side. (Or you may cook them on the grill or under the broiler.) To make coulis, process ingredients in blender and drain.

To Serve: Serve on burger buns, on slices of thick Italian bread or in pita pockets using Cucumber Coulis as garnish.

Quick and Easy: Substitute 2 10-ounce packages frozen vegetables for celery, carrot, onion, tomato and peas.

SERVES: 6	NUTRITIONAL INFORMATION PER SERVING		
Calories	331	Total Fat	3 g	Cholesterol	0 mg
Calories from Fat	8%	Saturated Fat	< 1 g	Sodium	659 mg

FAMOUS VEGETABLE SANDWICH

The textures and many flavors in this rich-tasting spread make it a delicious lunch choice.

1/2 pound firm tofu
1/4 cup Yogurt Cheese
  (see recipe on page 24)
1 tablespoon Dijon mustard
1 tablespoon soy sauce
  (or 1 tablespoon Worcestershire sauce)
1 clove garlic, minced
1 rib celery, chopped

1/2 teaspoon turmeric
1 tablespoon fresh dill, chopped
  (or 1 teaspoon dried)
1/2 cup carrot, grated
3 scallions, minced
salt and pepper to taste
4 pita pockets or whole-grain bread
lettuce and tomato

Drain tofu. In a medium-sized bowl, mash the tofu with a fork. Add yogurt cheese, mustard and seasonings. Add vegetables and lightly mix again. Chill. Salt and pepper to taste. Serve with lettuce and tomato on whole-grain bread or in large pita pockets.

SERVES: 4 — **NUTRITIONAL INFORMATION PER SERVING**

Calories	169		Total Fat	3 g		Cholesterol	< 1 mg
Calories from Fat	16%		Saturated Fat	< 1 g		Sodium	504 mg

TUNA MELT

6 ounces cooked fresh tuna
  (or water-packed canned
  tuna, drained)
1/4 cup low-fat cream cheese
1/2 cup peeled cucumber, finely diced

2 scallions, thinly sliced
1 teaspoon Worcestershire sauce
4 slices of crusty Italian bread,
  about 1 inch thick
2 ounces cheddar cheese, shredded

Flake tuna and blend with cream cheese, cucumber, scallions and Worcestershire sauce. Toast both sides of bread. Pile mixture onto two slices and sprinkle with cheddar cheese. Broil the two halves until cheese bubbles. To complete sandwich, top with a second slice of toast.

SERVES: 2 — **NUTRITIONAL INFORMATION PER SERVING**

Calories	183		Total Fat	2 g		Cholesterol	26 mg
Calories from Fat	8%		Saturated Fat	< 1 g		Sodium	336 mg

CALZONE

Here's a lightened-up version of an Italian favorite.

1 package (1/4 ounce) active dry yeast
1 cup warm water
1/2 teaspoon sugar
3 cups all-purpose flour, divided
1 tablespoon oil
1/2 teaspoon salt
non-stick cooking spray

12 ounces low-fat mozzarella cheese
2 ounces prosciutto, cut into strips
  (you may substitute Canadian bacon)
3 tablespoons chives, chopped
2 cloves garlic, minced
1 cup warm pizza sauce, for dipping

Combine 1 cup warm water with yeast and sugar in a medium-sized mixing bowl. Allow yeast to soften for 5 minutes. Blend in 1 1/2 cups flour and knead until smooth. Add oil and salt and gradually mix in remaining flour to make a firm dough. Knead until smooth and satiny.

Spray a large bowl with non-stick cooking spray. Put dough in bowl, turning to coat thoroughly with non-stick cooking spray. Cover with plastic wrap and then a damp towel. Allow to rise in a warm, draft-free place for about an hour.

Spray a large baking sheet with non-stick cooking spray. Knead down dough and divide into 6 pieces. On a lightly-floured surface, roll each piece into a 6-inch circle. Place 1/6 of mozzarella, ham, chives and garlic on each circle of dough. Moisten edges and fold over to enclose the filling, pressing the edges together.

Place on baking sheet and allow to rise again for about 30 minutes. Preheat oven to 375° F. Bake for 30 to 35 minutes or until the Calzone is browned. Serve warm with pizza sauce.

SERVES: 6	NUTRITIONAL INFORMATION PER SERVING				
Calories	324	Total Fat	6 g	Cholesterol	5 mg
Calories from Fat	17%	Saturated Fat	3 g	Sodium	481 mg

Shrimp with Artichoke Hearts - see page 140

Halibut with Confetti Sauce - see page 141

Ratatouille - see page 197

Red Beans and Rice - see page 200

Apple Dumplings - see page 209

Strawberry Tart - see page 214

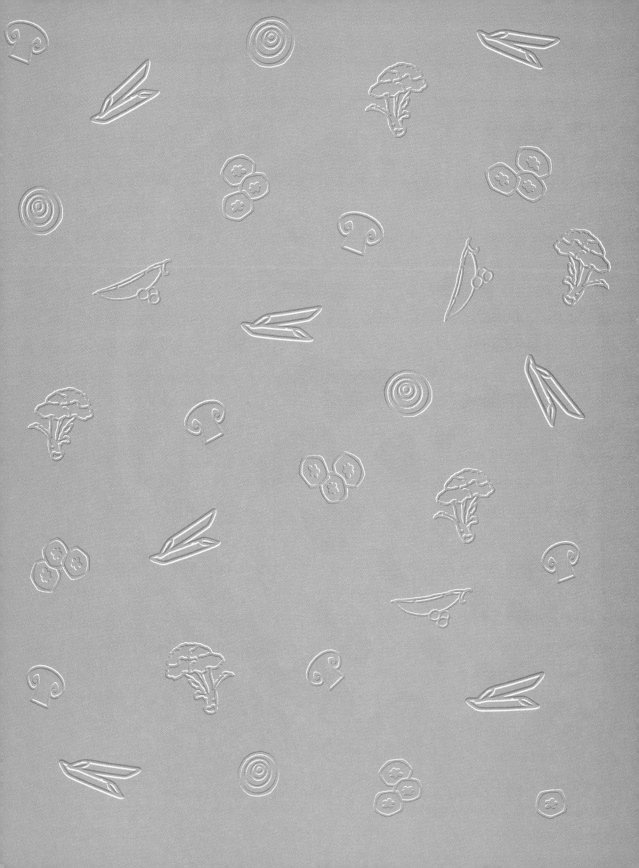

Pasta

It's difficult to think of another food that pleases as many different palates as pasta. Served with seafood or vegetables, meat or cheese, pasta is a great low-fat choice for even the busiest cook.

PASTA WITH FRESH TOMATOES

Fresh, home-grown tomatoes make this simple tomato sauce superior to any other sauce. In a pinch, canned tomatoes may be substituted.

4 large, ripe tomatoes, diced
  (or a 28-ounce can crushed tomatoes)
4 cloves garlic, sliced
2 tablespoons olive oil
1/2 cup basil leaves

2 tablespoons Italian parsley
salt and pepper to taste
8 ounces tubular pasta,
  such as rigatoni or penne, cooked
Italian parsley sprigs for garnish

Place tomatoes, garlic, olive oil, basil and parsley in a blender. Pulse several times or until sauce is smooth. Salt and pepper to taste.

Heat or serve at room temperature over hot pasta. Garnish with additional Italian parsley sprigs.

SERVES: 4 ══════ **NUTRITIONAL INFORMATION PER SERVING** ══════

Calories	283		Total Fat	5 g		Cholesterol	0 mg
Calories from Fat	15%		Saturated Fat	< 1 g		Sodium	21 mg

BOW-TIE PASTA WITH ZUCCHINI ASIAGO

The stewed squash gives this sauce its punch and the aroma is divine.

1 teaspoon oil
1 medium onion, cubed
2 cloves garlic, minced
1 teaspoon (or less) hot pepper flakes
2 zucchini, sliced and halved
   into half-moons
2 yellow squash, sliced and halved
   into half-moons

1/4 cup parsley, chopped
salt and pepper to taste
8 ounces bow-tie pasta, cooked
   according to package directions
1/4 cup asiago or other hard
   Italian cheese, grated
parsley sprigs for garnish

Heat oil in a heavy, non-stick frying pan. Add onion, garlic and hot pepper flakes and sauté until onions are translucent. Add zucchini and yellow squash and sauté until they just start to brown. Lower heat, cover pan and cook for 30 minutes, until zucchini stews and makes a thick sauce. Add water if sauce seems to be sticking to the pan.

Purée in a blender or food processor. Return to pan, add parsley and heat. Salt and pepper to taste.

To Serve: Divide cooked bow-ties among four plates. Top with zucchini sauce and asiago cheese. Garnish with additional parsley sprigs.

Calories	303	Total Fat	6 g	Cholesterol	15 mg
Calories from Fat	18%	Saturated Fat	3 g	Sodium	463 mg

CAPELLINI LA CHECCA

Literally, "a pasta for the common man," the trick to this simple recipe is to drench the angel hair pasta with the tomato water until all of the liquid is absorbed.

10 Roma tomatoes
   (or a 29-ounce can Roma tomatoes)
1/4 cup basil leaves, chopped
1 teaspoon salt
1 teaspoon pepper, freshly grated
4 quarts water

1 pound capellini (angel hair pasta)
2 cloves garlic, chopped
1 tablespoon olive oil
3 tablespoons Romano cheese
1 tablespoon butter

Chop tomatoes into 1/4-inch pieces. Blend with basil leaves, salt and pepper. Allow to stand for at least 1 hour or, preferably, 4 to 6 hours to allow the tomatoes time to "weep" and to form tomato water.

In a large soup pot, heat 4 quarts water to boiling. When water boils, add capellini and swirl it with a long fork for 2 minutes.

In a small, non-stick frying pan, sauté garlic in olive oil. Drain tomato water from tomato and basil mixture into a large bowl and, carefully, add garlic and olive oil to mixture.

Drain capellini and, with tongs, dip pasta into the tomato water. Continue to dip and swirl the capellini until all of the tomato water has been absorbed.

To Serve: Divide capellini among 4 large bowls and top with Romano cheese, butter and the tomato-basil dressing.

SERVES: 6 ═══ **NUTRITIONAL INFORMATION PER SERVING** ═══

Calories	372	Total Fat	6 g	Cholesterol	7 mg
Calories from Fat	15%	Saturated Fat	2 g	Sodium	465 mg

GNOCCHI WITH PROVOLONE

The secret to tender gnocchi is in blending just enough flour into the potatoes to achieve the right consistency.

3 large baking potatoes (about 2 pounds)	4 quarts water
1 to 1 1/4 cups all-purpose flour, sifted	non-stick cooking spray
1 teaspoon salt	6 ounces provolone cheese, sliced
	freshly ground black pepper

Preheat oven to 375° F. Prick potatoes with a fork and bake for 1 hour or until tender. Remove potatoes, cool slightly and scoop out flesh. Mash with fork. Cool thoroughly, allowing potatoes to dry out. Stir in only enough flour and salt so that the dough is smooth and elastic (the less flour, the more tender the gnocchi).

Roll into cylinders, 6-inches long x 1-inch diameter, and cut into 1/2-inch disks. In a large soup pot, heat 4 quarts water. Boil gnocchi for 5 minutes, until tender.

Preheat oven to 475° F. Spray a 9 x 9-inch square baking dish or pan with non-stick cooking spray. Arrange gnocchi in 2 layers with slices of cheese between. Grind black pepper over top and bake for 20 minutes or until golden brown.

SERVES: 4 ═══ **NUTRITIONAL INFORMATION PER SERVING** ═══

Calories	360	Total Fat	6 g	Cholesterol	26 mg
Calories from Fat	16%	Saturated Fat	7 g	Sodium	750 mg

LINGUINE WITH SHRIMP AND ARUGULA

A fiery pasta sauce with the delightful combination of tart arugula and tender shrimp.

1 teaspoon olive oil
1 small onion, chopped
1 clove garlic, halved
4 medium-sized, very ripe tomatoes,
  quartered (or 1 29-ounce can
  crushed tomatoes)
1/4 teaspoon (or less) cayenne pepper

2 cups arugula lettuce, divided
  (if not available, use spinach)
2 pounds medium-sized shrimp,
  in shell
1/4 cup parsley
8 ounces linguine, cooked al dente
  (2 minutes less than
  package directions)

Heat olive oil in a small, non-stick sauce pan. Add onion and garlic and sauté until translucent. Purée tomatoes in a processor with onion and garlic mixture. Return purée to sauce pan, adding cayenne pepper and 1 1/2 cups arugula.

Shell and devein shrimp. Add to tomato mixture with parsley. Cook just until shrimp turn pink, about 4 minutes.

When ready to serve, stir al dente pasta into tomato sauce and allow it to absorb flavors and finish cooking. Just before serving, add remaining 1/2 cup arugula.

SERVES: 4 ═══ **NUTRITIONAL INFORMATION PER SERVING** ═══

Calories	196	Total Fat	3 g	Cholesterol	196 mg
Calories from Fat	13%	Saturated Fat	< 1 g	Sodium	239 mg

LINGUINE WITH WHITE CLAM SAUCE

A quick and easy dinner that's tasty and satisfying.

13 ounces canned chopped clams
1 teaspoon olive oil
4 cloves garlic, minced
1 cup chicken stock
  (homemade or prepared)
1/2 cup dry white wine
1/4 cup parsley, chopped

8 ounces linguine, cooked
  according to package directions
4 tablespoons fresh basil
  leaves, shredded
basil leaves for garnish
1 tablespoon fontina cheese, grated

Drain clams, saving liquid. Heat olive oil in a large, non-stick frying pan. Add garlic and cook until just light brown. Add reserved liquid, chicken stock, white wine and parsley and heat to a boil. Boil and reduce broth to about 1 cup. Add clams.

To Serve: Place linguine on a large platter. Sprinkle basil over linguine and top with hot sauce. Sprinkle with grated cheese. Garnish with additional basil leaves.

SERVES: 4   **NUTRITIONAL INFORMATION PER SERVING**

Calories	297	Total Fat	5 g	Cholesterol	66 mg
Calories from Fat	16%	Saturated Fat	2 g	Sodium	111 mg

PASTA WITH MEAT SAUCE

A versatile sauce that may be used for pasta or as an all-purpose tomato sauce.

2 teaspoons olive oil
4 cloves garlic, minced
1 large onion, chopped
1 pound lean ground beef
2 16-ounce cans tomato sauce
1 28-ounce can crushed
  Italian tomatoes
1/2 cup dry red wine

2 tablespoons fresh oregano
  or marjoram, chopped
  (or 2 teaspoons dry)
1/4 cup thyme sprigs
  (or 1 tablespoon dry)
1/2 cup Italian parsley, chopped
hot red pepper flakes (optional)
1 1/2 pounds pasta, cooked

Heat oil in a very large, non-stick frying pan. Add garlic and onion and sauté until transparent. Add ground beef and cook until it has lost all red color. Drain any fat from pan. Add tomato sauce, tomatoes, red wine, herbs and hot pepper flakes. Simmer for 30 minutes, stirring occasionally.

Serve over pasta or use as an ingredient for other dishes.

SERVES: 10 ═══ **NUTRITIONAL INFORMATION PER SERVING** ═══

Calories	355	Total Fat	4 g	Cholesterol	29 mg
Calories from Fat	11%	Saturated Fat	1 g	Sodium	175 mg

PASTA E FAGIOLI

This popular Italian soup is a meal in itself.

1 tablespoon olive oil
1 large onion, chopped
2 cloves garlic, minced
2 ribs celery, sliced
2 carrots, cnopped
3 sprigs fresh thyme
   (or 1 tablespoon dry)
2 tablespoons fresh oregano,
   chopped (or 1 teaspoon dry)

1 28-ounce can crushed Italian
   tomatoes, with liquid
3 cups chicken stock
   (homemade or prepared)
8 ounces navy beans, soaked
   and cooked according
   to package directions
2 cups rigatoni, cooked
1/2 cup basil leaves or
   escarole, shredded

Heat olive oil in a large, non-stick soup pot. Add onion, garlic, celery and carrots and sauté until very tender. Add thyme sprigs, chopped oregano, tomatoes and stock. Cover and simmer for 1 hour.

Before serving, add beans and rigatoni and heat through. Serve garnished with shredded basil or escarole.

SERVES: 4   **NUTRITIONAL INFORMATION PER SERVING**

Calories	336	Total Fat	5 g	Cholesterol	38 mg
Calories from Fat	14%	Saturated Fat	< 1 g	Sodium	376 mg

PASTA WITH TOMATOES, MOZZARELLA AND BASIL

Here's a wonderful way to dress a fresh pasta sauce.

8 ounces pasta, cooked
2-ounces fresh (or baby) mozzarella
   cheese, cut into wedges

2 cups fresh tomato sauce
   (see recipe, Pasta With Fresh
   Tomatoes, on page 175)
shredded basil for garnish

In a large bowl, blend hot pasta with fresh mozzarella cheese. Allow cheese to melt.

To Serve: Place 1/2 cup fresh tomato sauce on each plate. Divide pasta among plates and garnish with shredded basil.

SERVES: 4 ══════ **NUTRITIONAL INFORMATION PER SERVING** ══════

Calories	292	Total Fat	6 g	Cholesterol	7 mg
Calories from Fat	18%	Saturated Fat	2 g	Sodium	53 mg

OPEN RAVIOLI WITH SCALLOPS

These little pasta sandwiches take some work, but it's worth it. If you don't have a pasta rolling machine, roll the pasta out by hand.

White Pasta:
1 cup all-purpose flour
1 egg
2 tablespoons water

Green Pasta:
1 cup all-purpose flour
2 tablespoons spinach purée
   (or you may use baby food spinach)
1 egg

Scallop Filling:
1 teaspoon butter
1 pound small scallops
1 cup dry wine
1/4 cup half-and-half
1 tablespoon cornstarch
white pepper
basil leaves

To make white pasta, blend flour with egg and a little water. Knead by hand or by food processor for 5 minutes. Wrap with plastic wrap and allow to rest for 30 minutes.

To make green pasta, blend flour with spinach and egg. Knead by hand or by food processor for 5 minutes. Wrap with plastic wrap and allow to rest for 30 minutes.

With rolling machine or with a rolling pin, roll out both pastas until thin and cut into 3 x 4-inch pieces. You may need a little additional flour if the dough is sticky.

There should be 8 white and 8 green rectangles. Cook pasta sheets in boiling water for 4 minutes and drain.

To make filling, heat butter to medium in a large, non-stick frying pan. Add scallops and gently sauté until just cooked, about 2 minutes. Add wine.

Blend half-and-half with cornstarch and whisk mixture into the wine to thicken slightly.

To Serve: Place 2 pieces of green pasta on each plate. Top with 1/4 of the filling and a dash of white pepper. Top each serving with two pieces of white pasta and garnish with basil leaves.

SERVES: 4		NUTRITIONAL INFORMATION PER SERVING			
Calories	384	Total Fat	7 g	Cholesterol	152 mg
Calories from Fat	16%	Saturated Fat	3 g	Sodium	236 mg

MACARONI AND CHEESE

An enduring favorite that especially appeals to children.

1 pound macaroni
1 cup 1% buttermilk
2 cups nonfat cottage cheese
non-stick cooking spray

1 1/2 cups low-fat cheddar
  cheese, sliced
1/2 cup low-fat mozzarella
  cheese, shredded
1/4 cup parmesan cheese, grated

Cook macaroni according to package directions. While macaroni cooks, blend together buttermilk and cottage cheese.

Preheat oven to 350° F. Spray a 9 x 13 x 2-inch casserole dish with non-stick cooking spray. Return cooked and drained macaroni to cooking pan. Blend with cheddar and mozzarella cheese until cheese has melted. Add buttermilk mixture and stir through. Pour into prepared casserole dish, top with parmesan cheese and bake until browned and bubbly, about 30 minutes.

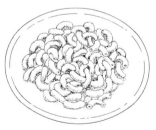

SERVES: 6		NUTRITIONAL INFORMATION PER SERVING			
Calories	451	Total Fat	9 g	Cholesterol	16 mg
Calories from Fat	18%	Saturated Fat	3 g	Sodium	418 mg

PASTA WITH SPINACH AND CHICKEN

This recipe is ready in just 45 minutes.

1 teaspoon red pepper flakes
1 teaspoon olive oil
2 cloves garlic, minced
1 pound fresh spinach,
  washed and stemmed

8 plum tomatoes, chopped
  (or 2 cups canned, crushed tomatoes)
1 whole chicken breast, with skin,
  about 1 pound
4 cups cooked pasta
1/2 cup fresh basil, chopped

In a heavy, non-stick soup pot, brown red pepper flakes in hot oil. Add garlic, stirring so that it does not burn. Add spinach in batches, cooking it down.

Add tomatoes and chicken breast. Cover and simmer for 30 minutes. Take chicken breast from pot. Remove skin and bones, slice and add back to spinach-tomato mixture.

Stir cooked pasta into spinach-tomato sauce with fresh basil. Serve on a large, heated platter garnished with additional basil.

SERVES: 4 ══════ **NUTRITIONAL INFORMATION PER SERVING** ══════

Calories	266	Total Fat	5 g	Cholesterol	69 mg
Calories from Fat	17%	Saturated Fat	1 g	Sodium	212 mg

RIGATONI IN FRESH TOMATO SAUCE
WITH SHELLFISH

Be careful to really scrub the shellfish so that sand doesn't get into the sauce.

1 dozen mussels, scrubbed and washed
1 dozen clams, scrubbed and washed
1 gallon water
2 tablespoons cornmeal
2 cups fresh tomato sauce
  (see recipe, Pasta With Fresh
  Tomatoes, on page 175)

1/2 pound mushrooms, sliced
1 cup dry white wine
1/2 pound bay or sea scallops
1 pound rigatoni, cooked
  according to package directions

Scrub clams and mussels, removing beards from mussels and discarding any clams or mussels that have opened. Soak for 1 hour in 1 gallon water with 2 tablespoons cornmeal to remove any excess sand.

Heat fresh tomato sauce. Add mushrooms, clams and mussels, cooking until shellfish open, about 5 minutes. Remove shellfish and keep them warm.

Add white wine to sauce, heat and add scallops. Allow them to cook until just tender, about 5 to 8 minutes depending on their size.

To Serve: Portion rigatoni onto plates. Top with clams, mussels and the scallop sauce.

SERVES: 8 ======= **NUTRITIONAL INFORMATION PER SERVING** =======

Calories	453	Total Fat	7 g	Cholesterol	122 mg
Calories from Fat	13%	Saturated Fat	< 1 g	Sodium	612 mg

TORTELLINI IN FRESH TOMATO SAUCE

Any stuffing will work in these tortellini – a little piece of sharp cheese, a little bit of meatball or this wonderful stuffing.

Stuffing
8 ounces ground turkey breast
5 sage leaves, minced
2 ounces Canadian bacon, minced
1 slice white bread soaked in milk

Sauce
2 cups fresh tomato sauce
  (see recipe, Pasta With Fresh
  Tomatoes, on page 175)
parmesan cheese to taste

Dough
3 cups all-purpose flour
2 eggs
1/2 teaspoon salt
1/4 cup water

To make stuffing, blend turkey breast with chopped sage, Canadian bacon and the bread drained of excess liquid. The mixture will be a little sticky, but you should be able to form 48 tiny meat balls. Refrigerate.

To make tortellini dough, blend flour with eggs and salt. You may mix this by hand or with an electric mixer or food processor. Add 1/4 cup or more water to make a smooth dough. Allow to rest for 10 minutes.

Cut into 4 parts. With a rolling pin or a pasta roller, roll dough thin. Cut into 2-inch circles with a biscuit or cookie cutter. There should be 48 circles. Cover circles with a damp towel.

To make tortellini, place a tiny meatball inside each circle of dough. Fold into the shape of a half-moon then fold over to seal filling. Fold ends together, twisting. Place finished tortellini onto a plate.

At this point, tortellini may be wrapped and frozen for up to 1 month or prepared immediately.

To prepare, heat a large soup pot with 2 quarts water to boil. Add tortellini and cook for 3 to 5 minutes, until dough is just tender.

To Serve: Place 1/3 cup fresh tomato sauce on each plate. Arrange 8 tortellini over sauce and dust with parmesan cheese.

SERVES: 6 ═══════════ **NUTRITIONAL INFORMATION PER SERVING** ═══════════

Calories	281	Total Fat	5 g	Cholesterol	108 mg
Calories from Fat	15%	Saturated Fat	1 g	Sodium	392 mg

SHELLS STUFFED WITH EGGPLANT PARMESAN

Easy to make, Eggplant Parmesan makes a delicious stuffing for the tender shells.

2 small eggplants (or 1 large),
  about 2 pounds
1/2 cup seasoned bread crumbs
1/4 cup parmesan cheese, grated
2 tablespoons basil, shredded
3 cloves garlic, minced
16 large stuffing shells
  (about 12 ounces), cooked half
  the time directed on package

non-stick cooking spray
1/4 cup low-fat mozzarella
  cheese, shredded
2 cups fresh tomato sauce
  (see recipe, Pasta With Fresh
  Tomatoes, on page 175)
basil leaves for garnish

Heat oven to 400° F. Prick eggplant with a fork and bake until very soft inside, about 30 minutes for small, 45 minutes for large. Cool. Scoop interior into a medium-sized bowl. There should be about 4 cups.

Blend with bread crumbs, parmesan cheese, basil and garlic. Divide among shells. Spray a baking dish with non-stick cooking spray. Layer shells into the dish, sprinkle with mozzarella, cover with aluminum foil and return to the oven to heat for about 15 minutes.

To Serve: On each plate, place 1/4 cup sauce, 2 shells and basil as a garnish.

SERVES: 8 ═══════════ **NUTRITIONAL INFORMATION PER SERVING** ═══════════

Calories	265	Total Fat	4 g	Cholesterol	3 mg
Calories from Fat	15%	Saturated Fat	1 g	Sodium	159 mg

VEGETABLE LASAGNA

Cook noodles and all vegetables in advance, then make white sauce, grate cheese and assemble.

1 tablespoon butter
2 cloves garlic, minced
3 cups nonfat milk
4 tablespoons cornstarch
1/2 cup basil leaves, chopped
non-stick cooking spray
1/2 pound lasagna noodles, cooked
   according to package directions

1 bunch asparagus, tips only, steamed
1 pound zucchini, sliced and steamed
1 10-ounce package tiny peas, steamed
1 red pepper, sliced and steamed
1/4 cup parmesan cheese, grated
1/2 cup low-fat mozzarella
   cheese, shredded

Preheat oven to 400° F. In a small saucepan, heat butter and sauté garlic. In a small bowl, whisk milk and cornstarch, then add to butter, whisking to make a medium white sauce. Add basil.

Spray a 9 x 13 x 2-inch casserole with non-stick cooking spray. Place 3 cooked noodles in dish and top with 1/3 of the vegetables, 1/3 of the sauce, a dusting of parmesan cheese and 1/3 of mozzarella cheese. Repeat for 2 remaining layers ending with a noodle layer. Top noodle layer with remaining parmesan cheese. Cover with aluminum foil and bake for 20 minutes. Uncover and bake until lasagna is browned, about 10 minutes.

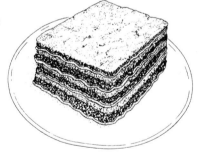

SERVES: 6 ══════ **NUTRITIONAL INFORMATION PER SERVING** ══════

Calories	319	Total Fat	7 g	Cholesterol	9 mg
Calories from Fat	19%	Saturated Fat	4 g	Sodium	270 mg

Vegetarian & Side Dishes

The dishes in this chapter use a variety of grains, beans, starchy and non-starchy vegetables. Vegetarians may want to adapt recipes that call for meat stock by using wine, vegetable stock (see recipe on page 59) or water. Cheese is optional in these recipes, so vegans may simply eliminate it. Discover the palate-pleasing surprises in this group of recipes – they are definitely not to be missed.

CARIBBEAN-STYLE BLACK BEANS AND RICE

Black beans and rice make an excellent main course or side dish. The flavorful blend of vegetables, lime, herbs and spices give this particular recipe added zing.

12 ounces black beans
5 cups vegetable or chicken stock
  (homemade or prepared)
1 tablespoon olive oil
1 large onion, chopped
2 green peppers, seeded and chopped
  into 1/2-inch chunks
2 cloves garlic, minced

1/4 teaspoon ground oregano
1 bay leaf
1 1/2 teaspoons ground cumin
1/4 cup lime juice
3 cups cooked rice
6 lime wedges for garnish
salt and freshly ground pepper to taste

In a large bowl, cover beans with water and soak overnight. Drain beans and place in a large soup pot. Cover with stock. Heat to a boil.

Meanwhile, in a large, non-stick frying pan, heat olive oil and sauté the onion, green pepper and garlic. Carefully add these vegetables to hot beans with oregano, bay leaf and cumin. Cover, lower heat to a simmer and cook about 1 hour, until beans are tender and soup is thick.

Just before serving, add lime juice and salt to taste.

To Serve: Divide rice among six large soup bowls. Add bean soup and garnish with a lime wedge and freshly ground pepper.

SERVES: 6	NUTRITIONAL INFORMATION PER SERVING				
Calories	226	Total Fat	4 g	Cholesterol	0 mg
Calories from Fat	14%	Saturated Fat	< 1 g	Sodium	16 mg

EGGPLANT PARMIGIANA

A delicious, crisp crust covers slices of savory eggplant.

1 large eggplant (2 pounds)
2 teaspoons salt
1 cup all-purpose flour
1 cup seasoned bread crumbs
1/4 cup parmesan cheese, grated
2 cloves garlic, minced
1 egg

4 egg whites
2 tablespoons oil
non-stick cooking spray
1/2 cup mozzarella cheese, shredded
6 cups cooked spaghetti
4 cups spaghetti sauce (homemade
   or prepared), heated through

Peel eggplant and slice into 1/2-inch slices. Sprinkle both sides with salt, place in colander and weigh down with plates. This will draw out the moisture, which is important to remove bitterness and to help the coating adhere.

Put flour into a shallow bowl. Blend bread crumbs, parmesan cheese and garlic in another shallow bowl. Beat egg with egg whites in a third shallow bowl.

Heat oil in a large, non-stick frying pan. Meanwhile, rinse salt from eggplant and pat dry with a paper towel. Coat all slices first with egg, then flour and finally bread crumb mixture. Sauté, a few slices at a time, in the non-stick pan until both sides are browned.

Preheat oven to 375° F. Coat a baking sheet with non-stick cooking spray. Place eggplant slices on baking sheet, sprinkle with mozzarella cheese and bake about 15 minutes, until cheese is melted and eggplant is tender.

To Serve: Divide spaghetti among warmed plates. Top with sauce, then eggplant slices. Serve immediately.

SERVES: 6 ══════ **NUTRITIONAL INFORMATION PER SERVING** ══════

Calories	442	Total Fat	9 g	Cholesterol	39 mg
Calories from Fat	18%	Saturated Fat	2 g	Sodium	294 mg

FALAFEL

Falafel combines potatoes and garbanzo beans, two excellent sources of fiber. Cooked falafel may be stored in the refrigerator for 3 days or in the freezer for 2 weeks. Add Hummus (see recipe on page 28) to the pita pocket for a great taste!

1 teaspoon plus 2 tablespoons olive oil	1/2 cup cilantro or parsley, chopped
2 cloves garlic, minced	1/4 cup nonfat yogurt
1 medium onion, chopped	1/4 teaspoon cayenne pepper
3 cups canned garbanzo (or cici) beans; 24 ounces, drained	1 teaspoon paprika
	juice of 1 lemon
1 large potato, cooked and mashed with nonfat milk	4 whole pitas, halved
	lettuce and tomato

In a medium-sized, non-stick frying pan, brown garlic and onion in teaspoon olive oil. Mash the garbanzo beans with a fork or purée in food processor with some of their liquid. Add to browned vegetables. Add the potato, cilantro or parsley, yogurt, cayenne pepper, paprika and lemon juice. Blend thoroughly. Chill for at least 1 hour.

Preheat oven to 350° F. Form into 24 balls, using about 2 to 2 1/2 tablespoons mix for each ball. Place on baking sheet and bake for 15 minutes.

Heat 2 tablespoons olive oil in a large, non-stick skillet. Sauté the falafel, a few at a time, until well browned on all sides.

Serve hot in halved pita pockets with shredded lettuce and tomato.

SERVES: 8 ═══════════ **NUTRITIONAL INFORMATION PER SERVING** ═══════════

Calories	182	Total Fat	4 g	Cholesterol	< 1 mg
Calories from Fat	20%	Saturated Fat	< 1 g	Sodium	455 mg

RATATOUILLE

A traditional vegetarian dish with a little added spice (see color photo on page 168).

1 large eggplant, about 2 pounds
1 teaspoon salt
2 tablespoons olive oil
2 large onions, chopped
4 cloves garlic, chopped
1 red pepper, seeded and diced
1 green pepper, seeded and diced

1 small zucchini, sliced
1 yellow squash, sliced
5 large tomatoes, peeled and wedged
2 tablespoons capers with liquid
1 large bunch Italian parsley, chopped
salt and freshly ground black pepper
   to taste

Peel eggplant and slice into 1/2-inch slices. Sprinkle both sides with salt, place in colander and weigh down with plates. This will draw out the moisture, which is important to remove bitterness and to help the flavors penetrate the eggplant.

Rinse salt from eggplant and pat dry with a paper towel.

Heat oil in a heavy, non-stick soup pot. Add onion and garlic and sauté until soft. Add peppers and cook until they are tender, about 15 minutes. Cube eggplant and add to pot with zucchini, yellow squash and tomatoes.

Simmer for 20 minutes to thicken and blend flavors. Add capers and parsley and cook for an additional 5 minutes. Salt to taste.

Serve in bowls with a sprinkle of black pepper and some crusty French bread.

SERVES: 6 ════ **NUTRITIONAL INFORMATION PER SERVING** ════

Calories	65	Total Fat	1 g	Cholesterol	4 mg
Calories from Fat	15%	Saturated Fat	< 1 g	Sodium	68 mg

PIEROGIS WITH POTATO-CHEESE FILLING

Once you get the knack of filling these delightful little packages, try other fillings such as sauerkraut, steamed broccoli with a little cheddar or your own leftovers.

Dough
4 cups flour
1 teaspoon salt
2 eggs
3/4 to 1 cup (more or less) water

Mashed Potato/Cheese Filling
2 cups firm, hot, mashed potatoes
2 tablespoons 1% buttermilk
1/4 cup processed cheese
1 tablespoon chives, chopped
salt and pepper to taste
4 cups water
2 tablespoons olive oil
1 cup onions, chopped
2 cups low-fat Yogurt Cheese,
  (see recipe on page 24)
1/2 teaspoon paprika

To make dough, mix flour and salt in a large bowl, making a well in center. Blend eggs with 3/4 cup water and add to flour. Work lightly with hands to form a firm, non-sticky dough. If necessary, use more water.

With a rolling pin, roll the dough to a 1/2-inch thickness on a floured board. Cut into 24 3-inch circles. Store in refrigerator with waxed paper between circles.

To make filling, blend mashed potatoes, buttermilk, cheese and chives. Salt and pepper to taste. Remove dough from refrigerator and place 1 tablespoon mixture onto the bottom half of each circle. Fold over to form a semi-circle, then crimp edges with a fork to seal.

In a large pan, heat 4 cups water to boiling. Add pierogis and boil until dough is tender, about 10 minutes. Drain and cool.

Heat oil in a large, non-stick frying pan. Add pierogis and onions, a few at a time, and lightly brown.

To Serve: Place 4 pierogis on a warmed plate topped with 1/3 cup yogurt cheese and a dusting of paprika.

Quick and Easy: Use premade won ton wrappers instead of making dough.

SERVES: 6	NUTRITIONAL INFORMATION PER SERVING				
Calories	503	Total Fat	11 g	Cholesterol	82 mg
Calories from Fat	19%	Saturated Fat	3 g	Sodium	548 mg

HERBED LEMON COUSCOUS

Couscous is a finely milled durum wheat that has been steamed and dried. Mint, lemon, scallions and garlic bring a Middle Eastern flavor to this wonderful grain.

1 teaspoon olive oil
4 cloves garlic, minced
6 scallions, sliced, with some green
3 1/2 to 4 cups vegetable
   or chicken stock, divided
   (homemade or prepared)

2 cups instant couscous, uncooked
1/4 cup chopped mint
juice of 1 lemon

In a medium-sized, non-stick saucepan, heat oil. Sauté garlic and scallions until soft. Add 3 cups stock and heat to boiling. Stir in uncooked couscous.

Remove from heat and let stand, covered, for 5 minutes. Sprinkle mint and lemon juice over couscous. Fluff with a fork, adding more hot stock if necessary. Serve immediately.

SERVES: 6	NUTRITIONAL INFORMATION PER SERVING				
Calories	157	Total Fat	2 g	Cholesterol	0 mg
Calories from Fat	11%	Saturated Fat	< 1 g	Sodium	10 mg

RED BEANS AND RICE

This recipe relies on the famous Cajun trio of onion, green pepper and garlic for a wonderful flavor (see color photo on page 169).

1/2 pound dry red beans (kidney beans)
4 cups vegetable or chicken stock
 (homemade or prepared)
1 large yellow onion, chopped
1 large green pepper, chopped
3 ribs celery, chopped

2 cloves garlic, minced
2 bay leaves
1 tablespoon Cajun seasoning
2 cups cooked rice
salt and freshly ground pepper to taste

Cover beans with cold water and soak overnight.

Drain the beans. In a large, non-stick soup pot, heat vegetable stock. Add beans, onion, pepper, celery, garlic, bay leaves and Cajun seasoning. Bring to a boil, reduce heat, cover and simmer for 1 hour. Continue cooking beans until tender. Watch the pot carefully to prevent the beans from scorching. Add water to pot as needed to make a thick bean sauce. When beans are tender, remove bay leaves. Salt to taste.

To Serve: Divide rice among 4 large bowls. Pour beans over each serving and sprinkle with freshly ground black pepper.

SERVES: 4 ══════ **NUTRITIONAL INFORMATION PER SERVING** ══════

Calories	224	Total Fat	1 g	Cholesterol	0 mg
Calories from Fat	6%	Saturated Fat	< 1 g	Sodium	44 mg

SPINACH LASAGNA

This deliciously healthy recipe makes a stunning presentation.

non-stick cooking spray
1 tablespoon olive oil
1 large onion, chopped
2 cloves garlic, minced
1 pound spinach,
    washed 3 times to remove sand
1 teaspoon oregano leaves
1 tablespoon fresh basil,
    chopped (or 1 teaspoon dried)

3 cups spaghetti sauce
    (homemade or prepared)
8 ounces whole-wheat lasagna
    noodles, cooked according to
    package directions
1/2 cup part-skim mozzarella
    cheese, shredded
1/4 cup parmesan cheese, grated
1 cup low-fat cottage cheese

Preheat oven to 375° F. Spray an 8 x 8-inch baking dish with non-stick cooking spray.

In a large, non-stick saucepan, sauté onion and garlic in oil until vegetables are translucent. Add spinach 1/3 at a time. Cover. As spinach cooks down, add more spinach. With last batch of spinach, add oregano, basil and spaghetti sauce. Blend thoroughly and remove from heat.

In the bottom of the baking dish, place 1 cup sauce. Place 1/3 noodles on top. Cover with 1 cup sauce and 1/3 of cheeses. Repeat 2 times, ending with cheese attractively sprinkled on top of sauce.

Bake for 40 minutes or until cheeses are well browned.

SERVES: 6 ═══ **NUTRITIONAL INFORMATION PER SERVING** ═══

Calories	287	Total Fat	6 g	Cholesterol	5 mg
Calories from Fat	18%	Saturated Fat	3 g	Sodium	438 mg

SUPER BURRITO

An expansive ingredient list makes this burrito truly "super."

5 1/2 cups vegetable stock
2 cups pinto beans
2 cups brown rice
2 Anaheim (or other mild) chilies
1 tablespoon olive oil
1 cup onion, sliced
1 cup green pepper, sliced
2 cloves garlic, crushed
2 teaspoons arrano (or other hot chili)
2 tablespoons chili powder
2 teaspoons cumin
12 whole-wheat tortillas

shredded lettuce and tomato
   for garnish
1/2 cup shredded Monterey Jack
   cheese for garnish

Cold Salsa
2 cups nonfat Yogurt Cheese
   (see recipe on page 24)
2 cups Roma tomato, chopped
1/2 cup cilantro, chopped
1/2 cup Anaheim chili, chopped

Soak pinto beans overnight and cook in vegetable stock for 2 hours. Add rice and Anaheim chili to bean-stock mixture. Simmer for 40 minutes.

In frying pan, heat oil. Add onion, green pepper, garlic and arrano chili. Sauté onions until transparent. Add chili powder and cumin.

Preheat oven to 350° F. Stir rice mixture into vegetable mixture. Divide mixture evenly among tortillas. Fold sides and roll so that burrito is enclosed. Place on a baking sheet and bake for 10 minutes or until tortilla is crispy. Meanwhile, make cold salsa by combining yogurt cheese with tomato, cilantro and chopped Anaheim chili.

To Serve: Place 1 burrito on each plate. Garnish with shredded lettuce, tomato, cheese and salsa.

SERVES: 12		NUTRITIONAL INFORMATION PER SERVING			
Calories	294	Total Fat	6 g	Cholesterol	9 mg
Calories from Fat	18%	Saturated Fat	2 g	Sodium	68 mg

VEGETABLE CURRY

Here's a hot, spicy and nutritious curry.

8 ounces dry navy beans
2 tablespoons oil
3 medium-sized onions, chopped
5 tablespoons Jalapeño peppers,
  chopped (optional)
2 green peppers, seeded and chopped
  into 1/4-inch pieces
1 red pepper, seeded and chopped
  into 1/4-inch pieces
1/4 teaspoon cayenne pepper
1/2 teaspoon white pepper
1 to 3 tablespoons curry powder

3 large, very ripe tomatoes, chopped
  (or 3 cups canned tomatoes
  with liquid)
1/2 cup frozen corn, thawed
  and drained
1/2 cup frozen peas, thawed
  and drained
1 stalk broccoli, stemmed and steamed
salt and pepper to taste
2 cups cooked rice
chopped apple, green onions and
  raisins for garnish

Soak beans overnight and drain. In a medium-sized saucepan, cover the beans with water. Bring to a boil, cover, reduce heat and simmer until beans are tender but not mushy, about 1 1/2 hours.

In a large, non-stick Dutch oven, heat the oil. Sauté the onions, peppers, cayenne pepper, white pepper and curry powder for 5 minutes. Add tomatoes and simmer for 10 minutes. Add the hot beans, corn and peas and cook for 5 minutes until vegetables are hot. Stir in broccoli. Salt and pepper to taste.

To Serve: Divide rice among large bowls. Pour curry over rice. Garnish with apple, green onions and raisins.

SERVES: 4 ===== **NUTRITIONAL INFORMATION PER SERVING** =====

Calories	408	Total Fat	7 g	Cholesterol	0 mg
Calories from Fat	15%	Saturated Fat	< 1 g	Sodium	68 mg

VEGETABLE ENCHILADAS

For best results, use hot chili beans or Mexican-style kidney beans.

non-stick cooking spray
2 teaspoons vegetable oil
1 medium-sized onion, minced
1 medium-sized green pepper,
   chopped into 1/2-inch pieces
1/4 cup fresh cilantro, chopped
2 cups frozen corn, thawed
2 cups zucchini, scrubbed and
   grated with skin on
1 15-ounce can hot chili beans
   (or Mexican-style kidney beans)
   with liquid

1 teaspoon cumin
1 teaspoon chili powder
12 corn tortillas
1 cup Tomato Salsa
   (see recipe on page 38)
3 ounces low-fat sharp cheddar
   cheese, shredded
3 ounces low-fat Monterey Jack
   cheese, shredded
salt and pepper to taste

Preheat oven to 350° F. Spray a 9 x 13-inch baking dish with non-stick cooking spray.

Heat the vegetable oil in a large skillet. Sauté the onion and green pepper until just tender. Add the cilantro, corn and zucchini and heat until zucchini is tender, about 5 minutes. Pour beans into a small bowl. With the back of a fork, mash beans in their liquid. Add to vegetables with cumin and chili powder. Stir thoroughly.

Soften the tortillas, if necessary, by wrapping in foil and placing in the preheated oven.

Place 1/3 cup filling in each tortilla. Roll tortillas up and place in baking dish. Cover with salsa and cheeses. Bake until sauce bubbles and cheese melts, about 20 minutes. Salt and pepper to taste.

SERVES: 6 ═══════ **NUTRITIONAL INFORMATION PER SERVING** ═══════

Calories	326	Total Fat	7 g	Cholesterol	11 mg
Calories from Fat	20%	Saturated Fat	1 g	Sodium	400 mg

VEGETABLE TACOS
WITH FRESH CUCUMBER SALSA

This recipe takes a little work but it is well worth the effort. The vegetable sauce reheats well and will last for 1 week in the refrigerator.

6 cups vegetable stock or stock made
   from 5 pounds pork bones
1 cup canned pinto beans with liquid
1 cup wild rice, uncooked
2 cloves garlic, minced
1 onion, chopped
1 stalk broccoli, cut into florets with
   stem peeled and chopped
12 taco shells
2 cups Fresh Cucumber Salsa
   (see recipe on page 38)

Yogurt Dressing
1 1/2 cups Yogurt Cheese
   (see recipe on page 24)
2 tablespoons dry white wine
2 tablespoons cilantro, chopped

In a large stockpot, heat vegetable stock, or cook pork bones for 1 hour in 2 quarts water and defat.

Add beans, wild rice, garlic and onion and heat to boiling. Reduce stock so that the mixture becomes the consistency of rich chili. Add broccoli and cook until just tender but still crisp.

To make yogurt dressing, in a medium-sized bowl, blend yogurt cheese with wine and cilantro.

To Serve: Place 1/2 cup bean-rice mixture in the center of a taco. Serve with yogurt dressing and *Fresh Cucumber Salsa.*

SERVES: 6 ═══════════ **NUTRITIONAL INFORMATION PER SERVING** ═══════════

Calories	228	Total Fat	5 g	Cholesterol	< 1 mg
Calories from Fat	19%	Saturated Fat	< 1 g	Sodium	191 mg

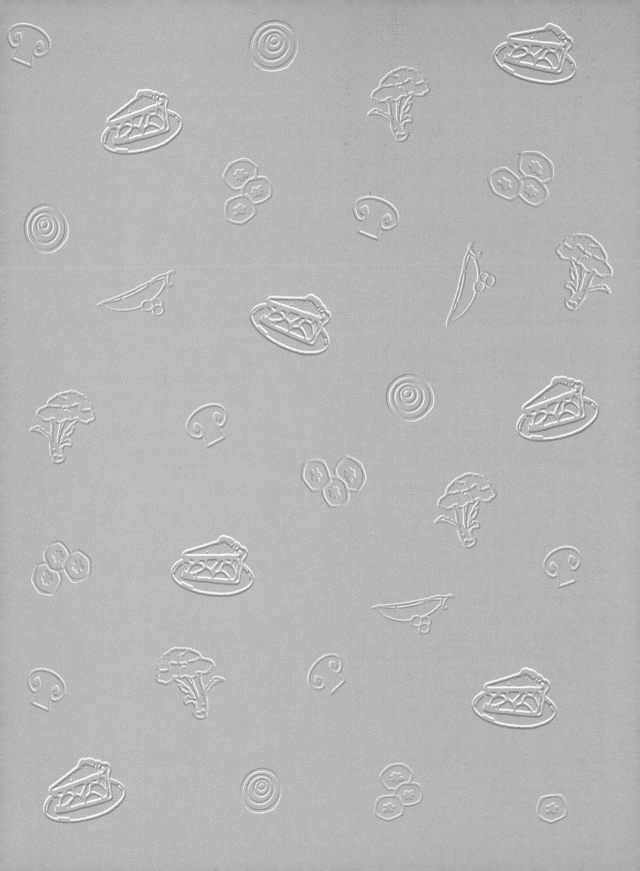

Desserts

The following luscious desserts are packed with flavor not fat, proving you *can* have your cake and eat it, too.

ALL-AMERICAN PEACH PIE

Here's a new twist on an all-American favorite. Great crust!

Pastry for 8-inch Double Crust
4 sheets frozen Filo dough, defrosted
  and wrapped in damp towels
non-stick cooking spray

Peach Filling
5 cups fresh peaches, pitted and sliced
  with skins (or a 20-ounce package
  frozen peaches*, not in syrup)
2 teaspoons lemon juice
3/4 cup granulated sugar
1/3 cup all-purpose flour
1/2 teaspoon cinnamon
2 tablespoons margarine

Preheat oven to 375° F. Remove a sheet of Filo dough from the damp towels. Double and place over an 8-inch pie plate. Spray a little non-stick cooking spray between layers. Repeat with second sheet of Filo. Trim to fit. Bake bottom crust for 10 minutes or until shell is golden brown.

In a large bowl, combine peaches with lemon juice. Add sugar, flour and cinnamon. Toss lightly to mix. Turn into prebaked bottom crust. Dot the  peach mixture with margarine.

Remove remaining sheets of Filo dough, double and place over the filling. Spray a little non-stick cooking spray between layers. Trim to fit and flute edges, sealing Filo layers. With a sharp knife, score the top of the Filo.

Place the pie on a large pan to catch any drips during baking. Bake the pie for 40 minutes or until the juice begins to bubble through slits in the crust. Serve warm.

*If using frozen peaches, increase flour by 1/4 cup.

SERVES: 6 ══════ **NUTRITIONAL INFORMATION PER SERVING** ══════

Calories	176	Total Fat	2 g	Cholesterol	0 mg
Calories from Fat	7%	Saturated Fat	< 1 g	Sodium	33 mg

APPLE DUMPLINGS

These sweet dumplings are a perfect finale to any meal (see color photo on page 170).

6 small-sized baking apples, cored
2 tablespoons granulated sugar
1/4 teaspoon cinnamon

Syrup
3/4 cup granulated sugar
1/4 teaspoon cinnamon
1/4 teaspoon nutmeg
3/4 cup water

Pastry Dough
non-stick cooking spray
1 1/2 cups all-purpose flour
1 teaspoon baking powder
1/4 teaspoon salt
1 1/2 tablespoons oil
2 tablespoons nonfat milk

To make syrup, combine 3/4 cup sugar with 1/4 teaspoon cinnamon and 1/4 teaspoon nutmeg in a small saucepan. Add 3/4 cup water, bring to boil and cook for 5 minutes. Set syrup aside.

Preheat the oven to 375° F. Spray a 9 x 9 x 2-inch baking dish with non-stick cooking spray. To make pastry dough, combine flour with baking powder and salt. With a pastry blender, cut in oil until the mixture takes on the texture of coarse crumbs. Add enough milk to moisten the mixture so that it will form into a ball. Allow the pastry ball to rest for 5 minutes. Divide into 6 parts. On a well-floured cutting board, roll each part with a rolling pin until it is approximately a 4-inch square.

Place an apple in the center of each square and sprinkle with 2 tablespoons sugar, blended with 1/4 teaspoon cinnamon. Wrap dough around apple, moistening and sealing edges so that apple is completely concealed in dough. Place in baking dish. Pour syrup over apple dumplings so that it completely wets them. Bake 45 minutes. Pastry will be crusty and apples tender. Serve hot or at room temperature.

SERVES: 6 ══════ **NUTRITIONAL INFORMATION PER SERVING** ══════

Calories	307	Total Fat	4 g	Cholesterol	< 1 mg
Calories from Fat	12%	Saturated Fat	< 1 g	Sodium	360 mg

ANGEL CAKE

A delicate, whole-grain cake with almost no fat and few calories. For a special treat, serve it with a tangy fruit sauce.

non-stick cooking spray

1/2 cup whole-wheat pastry flour
  (if pastry flour is unavailable,
  use whole-wheat graham flour)

1/2 cup cake flour, sifted

3/4 cup confectioners' sugar, sifted

12 large egg whites,
  at room temperature

1 1/2 teaspoons cream of tartar

1/4 teaspoon salt

1 cup granulated sugar

1 1/2 teaspoons vanilla extract

1/2 teaspoon almond extract

Preheat oven to 375° F. Coat a 10-inch tube pan with non-stick cooking spray. Blend pastry or graham flour with sifted cake flour and sifted confectioners' sugar. Set aside.

In a large mixing bowl, use an electric mixer to whip egg whites with cream of tartar and salt until mixture is foamy. Add sugar, 2 tablespoons at a time, 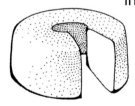 into egg whites, continuing to whip on high speed until stiff peaks form. Make sure all sugar has been incorporated into the egg white. (You can tell this by pinching a bit of the whipped egg white between your fingers; if sugar has been incorporated, you will feel no grains.) Fold in the vanilla and almond extracts.

Spoon dry ingredients, 1/4 cup at a time, into whipped egg whites. Fold in gently until just blended. Pour batter into the tube pan. Cut gently through the batter with a knife to remove any large bubbles.

Bake 45 minutes or until the crust is golden brown and cracks are very dry. Remove the cake from the oven and invert to cool for 1 hour. Loosen sides and bottom of cake from cake pan. Carefully remove cooled cake from pan.

SERVES: 12 ═══════ **NUTRITIONAL INFORMATION PER SERVING** ═══════

Calories	136	Total Fat	< 1 g	Cholesterol	0 mg
Calories from Fat	1%	Saturated Fat	< 1 g	Sodium	100 mg

CARROT CAKE

Carrot cakes are usually full of fat and sugar. This carrot cake is light, moist, delicious and low-fat.

non-stick cooking spray
2 cups all-purpose flour
1 cup granulated sugar
1 teaspoon baking powder
1 teaspoon baking soda
1 teaspoon salt
1 teaspoon ground cinnamon
1/2 teaspoon cloves
1 cup apple juice
3 cups carrots, finely shredded

1/3 cup light margarine
4 large egg whites

Cream Cheese Frosting
1 8-ounce package fat-free cream
   cheese, softened
2 tablespoons corn syrup
1 teaspoon vanilla extract
1 cup sifted confectioners' sugar

Preheat oven to 325° F. Spray a 13 x 9 x 2-inch baking pan with non-stick cooking spray.

In a mixing bowl, combine flour with sugar, baking powder, baking soda, salt, cinnamon and cloves. Add the apple juice, carrots, margarine and egg whites. Beat at low speed with an electric mixer until the ingredients are combined. Then, beat on medium speed for 2 minutes.

Pour into the prepared pan, pushing the batter a little higher around the edges than in the middle. Bake 60 minutes or until the center of the cake is firm to touch. Cool.

To make frosting, combine the cream cheese with the corn syrup and vanilla extract. Gradually add the confectioners' sugar and beat until smooth. Spread the cooled cake with the cream cheese frosting.

SERVES: 15   **NUTRITIONAL INFORMATION PER SERVING**

Calories	189	Total Fat	2 g	Cholesterol	< 1 mg
Calories from Fat	11%	Saturated Fat	< 1 g	Sodium	295 mg

APPLESAUCE CAKE

This is a very moist cake that is even better the second day.

non-stick cooking spray
3/4 cup raisins
2 1/4 cups all-purpose flour
1 teaspoon salt
1 1/2 teaspoons baking soda
1 teaspoon cinnamon
1/2 teaspoon ground cloves

1 tablespoon walnuts,
  toasted and chopped
1/2 cup light margarine
1 cup brown sugar, packed
2 tablespoons granulated sugar
1/2 teaspoon grated lemon peel
1 egg, beaten
1 1/2 cups applesauce

Preheat oven to 325° F. Spray a 10 x 10 x 2-inch baking pan with non-stick cooking spray. Plump raisins by steaming them over boiling water for 5 minutes.

Meanwhile, sift flour, then measure. Sift with salt, soda, cinnamon and cloves. Blend 1/4 cup flour mixture with raisins and walnuts.

In a large bowl, cream margarine. Add sugars and cream until well blended. Add lemon peel and egg.

Add flour and applesauce alternately to creamed mixture. When well blended, add raisin-nut mixture.

Pour into prepared pan, pushing the batter a little higher around the edges than in the middle. Bake 40 minutes or until a toothpick inserted into center of cake comes out clean. Cool in the pan for 10 minutes before removing.

SERVES: 12 ══════ **NUTRITIONAL INFORMATION PER SERVING** ══════

Calories	230	Total Fat	5 g	Cholesterol	18 mg
Calories from Fat	19%	Saturated Fat	< 1 g	Sodium	345 mg

FRUIT ICES

So easy, fruit ices are a tasty and light way to end a meal.

1 10-ounce package mixed
  frozen fruit with syrup
juice of 1/2 lemon

1/2 cup orange juice

Defrost frozen fruit. Blend with fruit juices in a food processor
or blender. Pour into 6 serving glasses and freeze until solid.

SERVES: 6		NUTRITIONAL INFORMATION PER SERVING			
Calories	114	Total Fat	< 1 g	Cholesterol	0 mg
Calories from Fat	1%	Saturated Fat	< 1 g	Sodium	4 mg

FRESH-FRUIT MOUSSE

1 envelope unflavored gelatin
1/4 cup plus 2 tablespoons
  water, divided
1/3 cup granulated sugar
juice of one lemon or lime

2 cups fresh fruit, such as strawberries,
  raspberries, or bananas
2 egg whites, at room temperature
1 tablespoon sugar

In a small saucepan, dissolve the gelatin in 1/4 cup water. Whisk until smooth.
Add sugar and stir until dissolved. Pour into a medium-sized bowl and allow
gelatin to begin to harden.

Meanwhile, purée fresh fruit, lemon or lime juice and 2 tablespoons water.
Whisk fruit mixture into gelatin mixture. Refrigerate for 30 minutes. Beat egg
whites until frothy. Sprinkle sugar over egg whites a little at a time, making sure
to incorporate all the sugar. Blend stiffly beaten egg whites into gelatin mixture.
Pour into serving bowl or into individual serving dishes. Refrigerate overnight.

SERVES: 4		NUTRITIONAL INFORMATION PER SERVING			
Calories	131	Total Fat	< 1 g	Cholesterol	0 mg
Calories from Fat	2%	Saturated Fat	< 1 g	Sodium	31 mg

STRAWBERRY TART

Here's a tart that will please everyone. It has a flaky crust, a sweet cream filling and gorgeous strawberries on top (see color photo on page 171).

Pastry for 9-inch Single Crust
1 to 1 1/4 cups all-purpose flour
1 teaspoon baking powder
1/3 teaspoon salt
1/4 cup oil
1/3 to 1/2 cup 1% buttermilk

Strawberry Cream Filling
3 egg whites
3/4 cup granulated sugar
3 tablespoons cornstarch
2 cups nonfat milk
2 teaspoons vanilla extract
1/2 cup currant jelly
1 quart firm, ripe strawberries,
    cleaned and hulled

Preheat oven to 400° F.

To make pastry, in a mixing bowl, thoroughly mix the all-purpose flour, baking powder and salt. Using a pastry blender, cut in the oil until mixture has a coarse texture. Sprinkle the buttermilk over the dough and blend until the mixture holds together well.

Wet the surface of the counter and place a piece of plastic wrap on the wet counter. Sprinkle plastic wrap with all-purpose flour. Place a ball of pastry on the plastic wrap and sprinkle with more all-purpose flour. Top the sprinkled pastry with a second piece of plastic wrap. Roll with rolling pin until the pastry is slightly larger than 9-inch pie pan. Remove one side of the plastic wrap and fit pastry into pie. Remove remaining plastic wrap. Bake 10 minutes or until crust is well browned.

To make filling, in a medium-sized mixing bowl, beat egg whites with sugar until just blended. Whisk cornstarch with egg whites a little at a time, to make a smooth paste.

Bring nonfat milk to just below the boiling point. Remove from heat. Dribble a small amount of milk into the egg white mixture, allowing it to heat. Add heated egg mixture into milk mixture, whisking to keep the sauce clear. Add vanilla extract and cool.

Spread 2 teaspoons jelly over crust. Pour filling into piecrust. Top with strawberries arranged in an attractive pattern. Coat strawberries with remaining jelly. Refrigerate until cool. Serve cold or at room temperature.

SERVES: 6		NUTRITIONAL INFORMATION PER SERVING			
Calories	316	Total Fat	< 7 g	Cholesterol	1 mg
Calories from Fat	20%	Saturated Fat	< 1 g	Sodium	196 mg

MERINGUE SHELLS WITH FRESH FRUIT

This elegant dessert is so delicious yet so low in fat.

1 piece 12 x 16-inch brown paper
  (a paper bag works fine)
6 egg whites, at room temperature
1/2 teaspoon cream of tartar

1/3 cup granulated sugar
3 cups fresh fruit
6 mint sprigs

Preheat oven to 200° F. Place brown paper on a baking sheet.

Whip egg whites with an electric mixer. Blend in cream of tartar. When egg whites are frothy, sprinkle sugar a teaspoon at a time over egg whites. Continue to beat egg whites until stiff, incorporating sugar well.

Divide into 6 portions on the paper. Make a well into each and bake for 8 hours.

To Serve: Carefully remove meringue shells from paper. Place onto small dessert plates. Spoon in fruit and top with a mint sprig.

SERVES: 6		NUTRITIONAL INFORMATION PER SERVING			
Calories	81	Total Fat	< 1 g	Cholesterol	0 mg
Calories from Fat	3%	Saturated Fat	< 1 g	Sodium	56 mg

RICE PUDDING

A pudding so smooth and rich tasting, it's hard to believe it's also low in fat.

1 cup brown rice, cooked according
   to package directions
1 cup evaporated skim milk
1/2 cup plus 2 tablespoons
   granulated sugar

1 teaspoon cinnamon
1/4 teaspoon allspice
1/4 teaspoon nutmeg
1 cup raisins
4 egg whites

Preheat oven to 300° F. Combine cooked rice with milk, 1/2 cup sugar, cinnamon, allspice, nutmeg and raisins. With an electric mixer or whisk, beat the egg whites until frothy. Add remaining sugar, a tablespoon at a time, and continue to beat the egg whites until soft peaks form. Gently fold the egg whites into cooled rice mixture, then pour mixture into a 9 x 9-inch square, ungreased baking dish. Bake 20 to 30 minutes until rice is set. Serve with fresh fruit or fruit sauce.

SERVES: 6		NUTRITIONAL INFORMATION PER SERVING			
Calories	276	Total Fat	1 g	Cholesterol	2 mg
Calories from Fat	4%	Saturated Fat	< 1 g	Sodium	91 mg

BLUEBERRY COBBLER

Blueberries work better than other fruits for this cobbler.

non-stick cooking spray
1 quart fresh blueberries, washed and
   drained
2/3 cup granulated sugar, divided
juice of 1 lemon
1 cup all-purpose flour
1 teaspoon baking powder

1/4 teaspoon salt
1/4 teaspoon allspice
1 teaspoon cinnamon
1/4 cup oil
1/2 teaspoon vanilla extract
1/2 cup low-fat milk
1 tablespoon sugar for topping

Preheat oven to 400° F. Spray a 2-quart baking dish with non-stick cooking spray. Spread the blueberries in the baking dish. Sprinkle them evenly with

1/3 cup of sugar and the lemon juice.

Blend flour with the baking powder, salt, allspice and cinnamon. In a separate bowl, blend the oil with the remaining 1/3 cup sugar and vanilla extract. Add the flour mixture to oil mixture alternately with the milk. Beat until smooth. Spread over the berries. Sprinkle top with 1 tablespoon sugar.

Bake 40 minutes until topping is well browned and center is firm. Serve warm.

SERVES: 6 — **NUTRITIONAL INFORMATION PER SERVING** —

Calories	258	Total Fat	5 g	Cholesterol	< 1 mg
Calories from Fat	15%	Saturated Fat	< 1 g	Sodium	249 mg

CHOCOLATE BANANA BROWNIES

Scrumptious brownies packed with nutrition and flavor.

non-stick cooking spray
4 tablespoons cocoa powder
3/4 cup water, divided
1 very ripe banana
1 cup granulated sugar

2 large egg whites
1 teaspoon vanilla extract
1/4 teaspoon salt
1 1/2 cups all-purpose flour

Preheat oven to 350° F. Spray an 8-inch round or square cake pan with non-stick cooking spray. Place the cocoa, 1/4 cup water and the banana into a large blender or into the bowl of a food processor fitted with a steel blade. Blend until smooth. Add the sugar, egg whites, vanilla extract and salt, blending until the mixture is smooth. Add the flour and 1/2 cup water, a little at a time, and continue blending until smooth.

Pour the chocolate mixture into prepared pan. Bake 20 to 25 minutes. Wait until the brownies have cooled before cutting into squares. Store brownies in refrigerator.

SERVES: 16 — **NUTRITIONAL INFORMATION PER SERVING** —

Calories	107	Total Fat	< 1 g	Cholesterol	0 mg
Calories from Fat	4%	Saturated Fat	< 1 g	Sodium	63 mg

INDEX